15 PRINCIPLES FOR ACHIEVING HAPPINESS

Also by Archibald D. Hart, Ph.D.

Feeling Free

Depression: Coping and Caring

Children and Divorce: What to Expect, How to Help

*The Success Factor: Discovering God's Potential
through Reality Thinking*

*Coping with Depression in the Ministry
and Other Helping Professions*

*The Hidden Link between
Adrenalin & Stress*

15 PRINCIPLES FOR ACHIEVING HAPPINESS

DR. ARCHIBALD D. HART

WORD PUBLISHING
Dallas · London · Sydney · Singapore

Unless otherwise noted, Scripture quotations used in this book are from The King James Version of the Bible (KJV). Other Scriptures are from:

The Living Bible (LB), copyright 1971 by Tyndale House Publishers, Wheaton, IL. Used by permission.

The New English Bible (NEB), Copyright © the Delegates of the Oxford University Press and the Syndics of the Cambridge University Press, 1961, 1970. Reprinted by permission.

The Holy Bible, New International Version (NIV). Copyright © 1973, 1978, 1984 International Bible Society. Used by permission of Zondervan Bible Publishers.

Library of Congress Cataloging-in-Publication Data:

Hart, Archibald D.
    15 principles for achieving happiness.

    1. Happiness. 2. Christian life—1960-
I. Title II. Title: Fifteen principles for achieving happiness.
BF575.H27H38   1988   158′.1   88-26123
ISBN 0-8499-0643

Printed in the United States of America

89 80 1 2 3 9 BKC 9 8 7 6 5 4 3 2 1

CONTENTS

ACKNOWLEDGMENTS

As with every writing project, there are many who contribute both directly and indirectly to its successful completion.

My secretary, Nova Hutchins, has faithfully typed and retyped this manuscript with charm and patience during a time of intense personal pain in her life. Her constant spirit of joy and deep commitment to her faith have been a profound witness to God's never-failing presence.

My administrative secretary, Bertha Jacklitch, has filled in every gap and covered every omission of mine during a busy time in the academic calendar.

And as always my wife, Kathleen, has coaxed and encouraged me throughout, providing valuable feedback and honest review of the manuscript as it progressed.

To each of these I say a very profound thank you.

Where Can I Find Happiness?

WHERE CAN I FIND HAPPINESS? This must surely be the most commonly asked question in every pastor's or counselor's office. It is certainly the question I hear behind every sigh or sob of anguish from my patients. If they are depressed, they want to know whether they will ever be happy again. If they are having conflicts at work or trouble with a spouse, they wonder whether happiness can be found in another job or another relationship— or even another town.

Where can I go to be happy—to be really happy? It's a question I have asked myself many times. Years ago I left the troubled land of my birth, South Africa, and came to the United States—to be happy. I became a faculty member at a seminary—to be happy. I'm beginning to plan my retirement (even though it is still some years away)—once again, to be happy.

Who doesn't want to be happy? That has to be the desire that dominates our minds—consciously or unconsciously—100 percent of every day. In fact, I think I could probably take every dream I have ever had, every spark of ambition I have ever exhibited, every friendship I have ever developed, and every penny I have ever spent—and interpret it in terms of my quest for happiness. There can be no more intrinsic ambition in life than the achievement of personal happiness.

As a Christian psychologist, I have been intrigued for many years with the problem of how to find genuine, abiding happiness. During the early period of my life, I convinced myself (and a few others) that there really was no such thing as happiness. "Your quest is all wrong," I would tell my quixotic self. "There are no phantom happiness knights out there to conquer—only rusty old windmills." I was convinced there were no real battles, no real challenges, no quests to complete that would give me real satisfaction. Happiness is a hackneyed word, overused and consequently so ambiguous as to be meaningless. It is only a fool's dream. Our life is too complex, and only the simple-minded think they can be lastingly happy.

Part of this pessimism about happiness stemmed from the fact that, like millions of others, I was raised in a dysfunctional home. (My parents divorced when I was twelve.) The tensions at home, then the pain and stigma of the divorce, led me erroneously to believe that I was not someone who deserved or could ever achieve real happiness.

Fortunately, at age eighteen I came to know Jesus Christ as my personal Savior, and after that my life began to change. I will never forget my first Christmas after I became a Christian. It was the most glorious Advent I have ever experienced: I opened up my mind and heart to the exquisite joy of being a soul set free. But nevertheless, my childhood had laid a damaging foundation for unhappiness. It would take many years before this damage could be undone and my newfound joy could become an abiding experience.

This book, then, rises out of the ashes of my own unhappiness. For I have learned that it *is* possible to be happy—deeply and abidingly happy. Happiness is not that elusive, and within all of us lies the potential for the enjoyment of life, especially our life in Christ. Recent research, as well as my personal experience and therapy I have conducted with scores of Christian believers, has helped me come to an understanding of what it takes to create happiness. I have also come to know, from personal experience, what destroys happiness. It is what I have learned about how to be happy and how to remove the obstacles to happiness that I hope to share in the pages to come.

HOW HAPPY ARE YOU?

Perhaps you have on rare occasions felt an overriding sense of emotional well-being, a "peak" experience. I suspect this has not happened as often as you would like. It's just as well, however, because we cannot build our expectation for happiness around these extraordinary ecstatic experiences. Life has to be lived in the valleys as well as on the mountaintops.

But is it unrealistic to expect that we can be personally happy most of the time? Is it the nature of happiness that it must always remain elusive and that its attainment is both mysterious and unlikely? Since most of life is a struggle, is it possible to create an abiding state of deep contentment that is more than a short-lived ecstatic experience?

Yes, I believe such happiness is possible. I believe that long-lasting, deep-seated, personal happiness can be achieved and that it is not so difficult to achieve as most might suppose. But it is like all habits—it must be *learned*. It requires *changes*. It demands *action* and *attention*. It can only be approached with *courage*. That's why so few people ever achieve it.

My assumption throughout this book is that you, the reader, would rather be happy than unhappy. Take heart, therefore, and journey with me as I share what I have come to believe are the basics for happiness.

But take a moment to rate your present level of happiness. Examine the "Happiness Scale" below which has ratings from zero to ten. A score of zero means you are "totally unhappy" most of the time, as miserable as you can imagine anyone to be. A rating of ten means you are "extremely and utterly happy," as happy as you imagine anyone could be if life were perfect. A five on the scale represents a "moderate level of happiness," where you experience a balance between sometimes feeling unhappy and sometimes feeling joyful.

Now rate your level of happiness by placing a small cross somewhere between 0 and 10 on the following scale:

HAPPINESS SCALE

0	1	2	3	4	5	6	7	8	9	10
Totally unhappy		More unhappy than happy			Balance between unhappiness and happiness		More happy than unhappy			Extremely happy

Remember your "Happiness Score" so that you can evaluate your progress.

Don't feel too bad if you have discovered at the outset that you're not a very happy person. You are in good company! Most people, especially if they are not following the principles outlined in this book, are generally unhappy. But very few would deliberately choose unhappiness if they could see a way to be happy. I have written this book because I believe that you (and I) could become happier by well-directed effort. I dedicate it, therefore, to be used together with God's grace to raise your happiness score.

ARCHIBALD D. HART

PART ONE

WHAT IS HAPPINESS?

"Most people are about as happy as they make up their minds to be."

Abraham Lincoln

"Happy is he that hath the God of Jacob for his help, whose *hope* is in the Lord his God."

Psalm 146:5, emphasis added

CHAPTER ONE

Is Happiness Possible?

THERE IS A LOT of unhappiness all around us. Personal happiness is not as common as you might think.

Ask yourself: "How many of my friends are really happy?" Then go down to a busy street corner or the entrance of your local shopping mall and study the faces of those hurrying by. How many look happy? And even if they're smiling on the outside, how many are deeply content within?

I suspect not many. Even though all of us have the capacity to be happy, few of us seem to achieve real and lasting happiness.

Dennis Wholey, the host/interviewer of the Public Broadcasting System television series, *Late Night America*, reports that experts he has interviewed (including psychiatrists, psychologists, educators, and religious leaders) believe that only about 20 percent of the American population is happy.* I'm surprised! I would have thought the proportion was much lower!

There is a lot of *apparent* happiness around us. People delude or drug themselves into what they believe is a state of happiness, when deep within they feel miserable—or at least uneasy, not at peace with themselves, their world, or their God. Solomon was quite right when he said: "Even in laughter the heart is sorrowful" (Prov. 14:13).

There are some who have plenty of reason to be unhappy. They are poor and impoverished, hungry and homeless, in ill health or suffering intolerable pain. Yet I have known such people to be extremely happy and deeply content.

Then there are those who seem to have every reason to be happy. They have all the worldly ingredients for happiness: money,

---

* *Parade,* 26 October 1986: 8.

power, success, good health, and full stomachs. Yet they are some-times among the most miserable of people.

And in between, hopefully, are you and I. We don't own a lot, but we have enough to get by with. We don't accomplish really great things, but we have a deep sense that there is some purpose for our lives—a fundamental meaning to our existence. We might even be believers in Christ's salvation and enjoy the benefits of prayer and spiritual renewal. But we *still* may not be personally happy!

Why is happiness so elusive? Happiness should be easy. But in reality it is not easy—for one important reason: Most of us don't know what happiness really is.

WHAT IS HAPPINESS?

Do you remember the bumper stickers that were popular some years ago? They began with the words, "Happiness is . . ." and they went on to make statements like "Happiness is being single," or "Happiness is being a fireman"—all intended to show that the person displaying the sign was happy because of certain condi-tions in his or her life.

I never really believed those signs! I always had a sneaking suspi-cion that the person who pasted such a sticker on his bumper was trying to hide his real feelings by claiming a happiness he didn't feel.

Still, I have to admit I've thought up a few "Happiness is" ideas myself, based on some situations I *wish* would happen. For in-stance: "Happiness is having a student confess that he didn't get an A because he didn't study!" or "Happiness is getting the top off a new aspirin bottle before the bottle disintegrates in the attempt."

But that brings us back to the question of what happiness is. Quite seriously, happiness is not just a matter of experiencing cer-tain conditions in life (such as being single or being a fireman). And it's certainly not just a matter of experiencing the impossible or receiving positive surprises (such as getting the top off the aspirin!).

So—what is happiness? Let's take a look at some more realistic ideas of what happiness is.

HAPPINESS IS . . . A CHOICE

Building a solid foundation for happiness is serious business. It doesn't just happen accidentally or by chance. It is more like a beautiful garden—you must plan thoroughly, cultivate carefully, and weed meticulously. You must pay attention to little details such as *how you think* or *what expectations you have* for your life. You must identify old unhappiness-producing habits and pull them out by their roots, just as you weed a garden.

No garden grows beautiful when neglected, and I would strongly assert that no mind produces happiness when left to grow by itself. Paul alludes to this fact in Philippians 4:8–9:

> And now, brothers [and sisters], as I close this letter let me say this one more thing: Fix your thoughts on what is true and good and right. Think about things that are pure and lovely, and dwell on the fine, good things in others. Think about all you can praise God for and be glad about. Keep putting into practice all you learned from me and saw me doing, and the peace of God will be with you" (LB).

As this passage of Scripture reveals, happiness is not an accident; it doesn't just fall into our laps. Rather, it results from a disciplined and deliberate effort. It is something that can be *achieved*. And the achievement of true happiness is neither esoteric nor mysterious. It is a habit of the heart and mind that one can *learn* and pass on to one's children.

In the ordinary course of life very few have legitimate excuses not to be happy. True, some diseases can destroy those parts of the brain that facilitate our feelings of well-being, and tragic experiences can temporarily suspend our mental tranquility. But eventually we have to adjust to and accept even the most devastating of life's blows in order to restore our basic happiness.

The fact is that, in the long run, we *choose* our misery—it is almost never imposed upon us. And conversely, happiness grows out of choosing to live harmoniously with your life circumstances—whatever they are.

In the chapters that follow, I will frequently beat this theme-drum. Happiness matures when we deliberately pursue attitudes of good will and tolerance as well as the understanding of love. If we turn our backs on these character-building virtues, then we select misery over happiness—and we have only ourselves to blame.

SCIENTIFIC EVIDENCE FOR HAPPINESS

But that brings us once more to our original question. If happiness is a choice—and if most of us would rather be happy than unhappy—why do so many people choose to be unhappy? Primarily because they are unaware of the basic principles that determine happiness. These essential ingredients of human happiness are simple and available to all. The trouble is, they are *so* basic that many people overlook or ignore them!

Interestingly enough, the idea that happiness is achievable by following certain basic principles is not just a philosophical or theological one. There is definite scientific evidence that personal happiness can be achieved—that the achievement of consistent happiness is something which is under our control.

While early psychological researchers questioned whether high levels of personal happiness should, or could, be developed, studies over the past twenty years have accumulated a vast body of information that not only shows that happiness *can* be achieved—but also outlines *how* it is best attained. Science now knows more than it has ever known about the attributes, personality, and characteristics of happy people.

The happiness research being conducted at a number of prestigious universities has revealed that a "sense of happiness," not just a short-term mood of ecstasy, results from a great many factors. While the interaction between these factors is complex and specifics not always easy to tease out, several clearly identified "principles" have emerged as foundational to happiness. These principles are quite simple and effective—in fact, therapeutic programs using "happiness-increasing techniques" have proven effective in enhancing the personal happiness of participants.

One series of studies identified more than a dozen fundamental characteristics of happy people.* These characteristics include keeping busy and active, doing productive work, spending more time with friends, lowering your expectations, and being yourself. Being aware of these basic characteristics can be very helpful in building a happy life. In the chapters to come I will elaborate on many of them and show how they can be incorporated into the life of an individual.

BUT WHAT ELSE IS NEEDED?

Almost sixty years ago, the renowned philosopher Bertrand Russell wrote a book entitled, *Conquest of Happiness*. In the

---

* Michael W. Fordyce, *Journal of Counseling Psychology*, 30, no. 4 (1983): 483–84.

preface he wrote, "It is in the belief that many people who are unhappy could become happy by well-directed effort that I have written this book." I share this sentiment—I am writing this book for the same reasons that Russell wrote his. But there are some important differences between our approaches.

First, the scientific world now knows a lot more about happiness than Bertrand Russell knew in 1930. I want to share some of those findings.

And second, Russell was an atheist—God played no part in his prescription for personal joy. While he acknowledged that "the happy life is to an extraordinary extent the same as the good life," he had no words of wisdom on how to live a "good" life.

I, on the other hand, make no apologies for my Christian bias. I believe true and complete happiness can *only* be found in the self's being reunited with its creator. To be deeply and lastingly happy, we have to love something and be loved by someone outside of ourselves. Better still, we need a God who indwells us through Christ and is a part of our every act, thought, or state of mind. To exist in a world without being reunited and living in harmony with one's creator brings misery as surely as winter brings cold. And we can never find real or lasting happiness while we live outside of God or in a state of rebellion against Him.

The principles of happiness identified in the scientific "happiness studies" can be very useful in helping us build a happy life. But even all of these principles together are still not enough to guarantee happiness—they are not enough to stake a life on. As helpful as science is, when it addresses the deep issues of life it cannot always measure or discern the truth. Certainly, God has established important limits as to how far the self can seek after its own fulfillment, so we need to be very clear about the boundaries God has established to our search for happiness.

I believe that, as we examine God's many prescriptions for happiness as found in Scripture, we will find a more satisfactory source of wisdom for living a "good" life than Bertrand Russell had to offer—as well as a more substantial basis for happiness than any scientific study can provide.

THE PRINCIPLES OF HAPPINESS

In the chapters to come, then, I will seek to share with you in practical ways the body of knowledge that has emerged from happiness research. Coupled with the grace of God, it offers you hope for a greater experience of joy than you are currently experiencing.

I will present fifteen principles that, if followed and incorporated prayerfully into your beliefs, attitudes and behaviors, will significantly increase your sense of emotional well-being. I have personally found them to be life-transforming; they have enhanced my spiritual growth as well as promoting psychological and physical healing in my life.

Let me emphasize, however, that the ideas I will be presenting are only *principles*—general behavioral prescriptions—and not rules of law. While I will provide many examples of how these principles can be applied, it is up to you to translate and apply them to your own specific life circumstances. Your success at "growing" your own happiness will depend on the sincerity and persistence with which you put these principles into practice.

But again, self-reliance is not enough. Follow the guidelines presented in this book. But at the same time, let God and His Spirit aid you every step of the way.

CHAPTER TWO

Causes of
Unhappiness

BEFORE WE CAN EXAMINE the principles that help build a solid foundation for happiness, we need to briefly look at some common causes of unhappiness. This will help us put our quest for happiness in better perspective.

Do you ever ask, in a moment of weakness, "What's wrong with God? Couldn't He have created us to be happy all the time?" Or perhaps you worded it this way: "Why does He allow unhappiness in His world?"

Frankly, I don't have answers to these questions. As a matter of fact, I suspect no one does! One of the great mysteries about God is that we cannot always discern His purposes. Like the other great questions of life—Why does God allow suffering? Why do we have to die?—The question of happiness is one we can only guess at. The human mind is limited in its understanding.

As believers we accept by faith that these dilemmas of human existence have a purpose, and we continue to live to the best of our ability despite the fact that we don't have perfect understanding. I know that God joins us in our suffering and can be closer to us in pain than in pleasure. I also know that most human unhappiness is brought on by our own stupidity and carelessness, so we shouldn't be too quick to blame it on God.

There are many causes of unhappiness. Some are *external*, or imposed from the outside, but most are *internal*, or created by ourselves. Some are easily discerned, such as anger and envy, while others are more subtle and hard to identify, such as being inauthentic or suffering from a lack of affirmation.

My later discussion of the specific principles for building happiness will touch on many of the subtle causes of unhappiness. But so that we don't overlook the obvious I will focus here on the more common causes of general unhappiness, with the hope that you

9

will identify these problems in your own life and resolve as many of them as possible *before* proceeding to apply the happiness principles. It's like weeding the garden before planting new flowers!

In this chapter we will look at four common causes of unhappiness—guilt, anger, selfishness, and fatigue. From my experience, these four seem to cover the problems of most of the people I encounter.

GUILT

As a Christian psychologist with much experience in doing psychotherapy with Christian patients, I would have to say that guilt heads the list of "causes of unhappiness." In our highly developed, technologically sophisticated, twentieth-century society, we don't seem to be able to receive forgiveness freely from God or from others. Scores of people live with a "conscience" that is harsh, unrelenting, and unforgiving. Psychologists call such unreasonable self-blame "neurotic" guilt, and it is rampant in our homes, churches, and workplaces. People who suffer from neurotic guilt feel a sense of wrongdoing that is out of proportion to the violation they have committed, and their psyches insist that they must be punished. At an unconscious level, such people do *not want* forgiveness, and they may seek the punishment they feel they deserve in many ways—from having "accidents" to becoming depressed. But in doing this, the sufferer also rejects the work of Christ on the cross, in which He came to bear the punishment for all our sins, real or imagined.

In becoming neurotically guilty, we create a strange paradox. We desire God's forgiveness for our sins, yet psychologically we expect punishment as the only way of restoring our inner peace.

How does this come about? Clearly the pattern of expecting punishment rather than forgiveness for our wrongdoing is laid in our childhood. When we are excessively punished, even by well-meaning and devoted parents, we come to expect punishment as the only way of resolving our guilt. We internalize this expectation and won't allow ourselves to "go free." Originally, the punishment comes from the outside, but we quickly learn how to create it from the inside. We learn to rob ourselves of any good feelings and create a state of unhappiness. We say to ourselves, "You are a bad person. You deserve to suffer." And we unconsciously force ourselves into feeling depressed and dejected.

When this pattern is maintained for many years, it becomes a deeply rooted habit that is very difficult to break. It can also become a significant obstacle to the gospel, since a person who suffers from neurotic guilt has great difficulty feeling God's forgiveness. Dr. Frank Lake, a British psychiatrist has even stated that the first task of the evangelist, is to help people resolve their neurotic guilt so that the "true" guilt of God's conviction can be more easily established. These are profound thoughts from someone who really understands the human condition!

Clearly, one of a minister's primary tasks is to help people distinguish between this neurotic form of guilt (which desires punishment) and God's real convictions. "True guilt" readily responds to forgiveness. It is an honest recognition of one's sins and failures before God, coupled with the realization that no amount of self-punishment can pay the penalty of this unrighteousness. Those who admit true guilt simply accept God's forgiveness and stop rejecting themselves.

A healthy "sense of sin" is very important to our psychological and spiritual health. But a sense of sin that brings with it no hope of forgiveness can destroy *any* basis for happiness.

Unfortunately, a neurotic sense of sin can be so deeply rooted in a personality that undoing it may require many years of counseling, as well as the patient understanding of healthy friends. Like many bad habits, the habit of unhealthy guilt is hard to break. But like other habits, it *can* be broken—and the results are worth the effort.

ANGER

Anger can take many forms. Sometimes it quietly eats away your stomach in the form of an ulcer. Often it finds its way into criticism and fault-finding. Other times it distorts the act of disciplining your children, turning the need to train them into a desire to punish them—or even into a strong need to get revenge for the hurt a child has caused you.

Clearly, anger can be destructive in terms of hurting other people. But anger always hurts the one who is angry as well as the person who is the object of that anger. It is a boomerang that returns with a great vengeance whenever you throw it out.

This is why *anger is bad for us!* Don't believe those who say that anger is a "positive emotion" or that anger is a "creative force" that drives us to accomplish great things. Can any verse of Scripture be clearer about what we ought to do with *all* anger than

Ephesians 4:31: "Let all bitterness, and wrath, and anger, and clam-
our, and evil speaking, be put away from you, with all malice"?

Why is anger so bad for us? Because it creates a unique state of
biological arousal which if allowed to exist unattended can be
extremely harmful to our systems. The increase in the level of
circulating stress hormones, if unchecked, can create high blood
pressure, ulcers, headaches, and the risk of premature artery
disease.

Now, what *is* good for us is to *know* when we are angry. To be
angry and not be conscious of it is probably the worst of all
emotional states. I believe that the *feeling* of anger is a sort of
warning signal, very much like a smoke alarm which warns us of a
hidden fire. The purpose of anger is to make known a grievance
or hurt. If we don't pay attention to the signal of anger, we could
very well be neglecting the grievance or hurt. If left unrecognized,
such hurts can accumulate and destroy our happiness.

Anger is designed to mobilize us to action whenever we are
threatened. To be angry and not be "in touch" with this anger
not only is very dangerous, but also robs us of an opportunity to
repair our damaged relationships. This is why therapists take a
lot of time in therapy helping patients identify their feelings of
anger.

But I disagree with many secular forms of psychotherapy in
what I believe we must *do* with our angry feelings. Whereas the
feelings of anger are legitimate and cannot always be avoided, I
don't believe anyone has the right to translate these feelings into
aggressive behavior. We have no mandate for this in Scripture. To
act out our feelings in angry behavior, attacking or humiliating
others, is not only destructive but downright unchristian.

Only God can take revenge (Rom. 12:19). *Only* God can punish.
All we have to give those who hurt us is forgiveness (Eph. 4:32).
This is the "genius" of our Christian faith. It is healthy, wholesome,
and conducive to happiness.

Now, I know that many readers will be asking questions like:
"But what about 'righteous anger'? Doesn't this lead to correcting
abuses? Are we not, of necessity, called to be angry at some situations in order to fulfill God's purposes in this world?"

My answer is quite simple. It is true that, for many of us, anger
is the only thing that gives us the courage to stand up for something right. It gives us the motivation to take corrective steps,
launch a campaign against injustice, or simply say "no more" to
some cruelty. The organization MADD (Mothers Against Drunk

Drivers), which has done so much to fight the deadly combination of alcohol and driving, is a good example of how anger can motivate us to worthwhile activities—MADD was begun by a woman whose daughter was killed by a drunk driver.

But quite frankly, it is unrealistic (and destructive) to expect people to maintain a high level of real emotional anger all the way through a campaign against injustice. Anger may initiate an action. Rage may motivate us against lethargy and get us moving. But rational, volitional action must take over to sustain genuine and productive action against injustices or evil.

Most "righteous anger" settles down not as a real gut-wrenching, body-destroying emotion, but as a mental attitude and awareness that keeps us motivated and directed at completing a course of action. Never use this sort of anger as a justification for a continuous state of destructive arousal.

SELFISHNESS

I do not know a selfish person who is happy, do you? I know that when I am selfishly preoccupied (and God knows how often this is), I am also at my unhappiest.

I also know that I am a lot happier at my present stage of life than at any previous time, for the reason that I have successfully reduced my desire for certain material things and have diminished my preoccupation with myself. I have come to accept that most of my shortcomings are no fault of my own, and I realize that to have the "courage to be imperfect" is not a weakness but a strength.

Excessive preoccupation with oneself never leads to a productive life. It causes one to become self-rejecting and unhappy. The "me-centered" Christianity so prevalent in our contemporary evangelical world is no exception.

Self-interest or selfishness can take many forms, and we have some interesting labels to describe them.

First of all, there is *hedonism*. A hedonist is a person who believes (and practices) the principle that happiness is to be found in seeking pleasure. The pursuit of pleasure, often at the expense of more wholesome pursuits, becomes the primary reason for living.

I know a man who went through a period of his life totally preoccupied with his search for pleasure. He rejected his wife and two beautiful children, dumped all responsibilities, and took off on a pleasure cruise. He spent many months in idleness, believing he "had earned the right to have fun" through years of "hanging in on his commitments."

When this man finally came to his senses, he was a miserable wreck—just like the prodigal son. He finally had realized that his so-called "freedom" was no freedom at all, and that he had been much happier when he had responsibility and commitment. But it was too late to recover what he had thrown away, and finally, in a bout of deep depression, he took his own life.

Of course, there is another side, or extreme, to hedonism— the inability to experience *any* pleasure. Often this occurs in people who are controlled by neurotic guilt. Their preoccupation with their apparent sinfulness and their continuous need for self-punishment robs them of any potential to let go and enjoy themselves. They engage life too seriously; they have no "inner child" that frees them to play.

These are the people who go to a church Christmas party and cannot allow themselves to have fun. They visit exotic places but feel so guilty for a little self-indulgence that they talk themselves out of luxuriating in their diversion. They take vacations but cannot allow themselves to rest or laugh. Why do I call them selfish? Because they are excessively involved in alleviating neurotic guilt. Such obsession then affects others by making *them* feel guilty when they enjoy themselves.

Another form of selfishness is *narcissism*, named after the young man in Greek mythology, Narcissus, who fell in love with his own reflection in a pool. People with narcissistic tendencies tend to have a strong sense of their own importance or uniqueness. They constantly need to feel successful, and they require attention and admiration from others. Because they have this exaggerated sense of self-importance, they create within themselves the unrealistic expectation of unlimited ability, power, wealth, or beauty, and they exploit others to gain their ends.

Unfortunately, their self-esteem is also fragile. Because they cannot always secure the love they so desperately crave, they easily become disappointed and unhappy. Their mood then swings from extreme ecstasy to shame, humiliation, emptiness, or rage.

To some extent our culture, including our Christian subculture, shapes us all towards narcissism. As many social commentators have noted, we are a narcissistic society, selfishly preoccupied with individualism and with success and self-glorification. Even many well-meaning believers are unknowingly caught up in this narcissistic self-preoccupation. Successful (and some not so successful) television ministries make this their main selling point. They thrive on the average person's craving for self-glorification through success and wealth, and without flinching they promise this to unsuspecting, well-intentioned believers. Is it any wonder, then, that we are also an unhappy people?

Coming right down to the street where you and I live, if we are going to be happy, we must begin by confessing that our selfish pursuits are not Christ-centered. And then we must seek to balance our ambitions with an appropriate concern for others. We live in community, and the whole body of Christ should be our primary concern.

Ralph Waldo Emerson put it in a nutshell when he wrote:

> To leave the world a bit better,
> Whether by a healthy child, a redeemed social condition
> or a job well done;
> To know even one other life has breathed easier
> because you lived:
> This is to have succeeded.

There is yet another form of selfishness that must be avoided because it also destroys happiness: *selfish self-denial*. This brand of selfishness is particularly bothersome because it poses under the guise of being "spiritual." It is the attitude that we must so obliterate the self in self-surrender or self-denial so as to count for nothing. "The self must die" is a notion bandied about in many Christian circles without much understanding of what it means. The result is that many become confused as to what they should or shouldn't do and how they should feel about themselves.

For believers there is a healthy "denying of the self." All love requires that we put someone else's interests ahead of ours. But this "denying" can easily become a selfish preoccupation. It *does* mean that we surrender our right to dominate others. It *does* mean that Christ has a claim on every part of our lives and that we are called to be obedient to His will. But what it does *not* mean is that we give others the right to walk all over us or that we become wimps or nonentities.

The self that must be denied is that part of the self Freud called the "id," or what the apostle Paul called the "lower" or "carnal" nature. It is that part of us that is the source of our passion, lust, and self-seeking pleasure. While this part of you cannot be destroyed (you would have to kill yourself to completely get rid of it), it must be brought under the control of the Holy Spirit by surrender of the self to God. We "walk in the Spirit" so that we do not "fulfil the lust of the flesh" (Gal. 5:16). We "put on" the Lord Jesus Christ and "make [no] provision for the flesh, to fulfil the lusts thereof" (Rom. 13:14).

Now note this very important point: We must *not* deny that part of the self called the *ego*, the "I" or "me." This part of the self is who I am. It is the "I" that lives in Christ and Christ lives in the "me." It makes no sense to speak of denying this part of me. It was worthy enough for Christ to die for and save, so it must be given liberty to become what He wants it to be. Selfish preoccupation with my own self-aggrandizement on the one hand and self-derogation or disparagement on the other are two extremes of dealing with myself that will only produce unhappiness. To live fully as myself, surrendering my lower nature to the control that Christ gives me through His power, claiming my heritage as His heir and assertively pursuing His will, will free me to live a happy and fulfilled life. I would even go so far as to say that this is the *only* way to real happiness.

FATIGUE

Fatigue is a much more serious obstacle to happiness than most of us realize. Most of us live hurried and hassled lives. We don't get enough sleep, and we seldom take sufficient time to relax and allow full recovery of our exhausted bodies and minds.

As I tried to show in my book *Adrenalin & Stress,* * most of us are "adrenalin addicts." We are hooked on an elevated level of our own stress hormones, and we constantly seek a "high" from some thrill or challenge. Whenever we "let down," we go into a post-adrenalin withdrawal depression. It's like the feeling of anticlimax after a period of excitement. This roller-coaster lifestyle leaves us in a chronic state of fatigue that is definitely not conducive to happiness.

Fatigue can take many forms. Sometimes it is physical. Sometimes it is emotional. It can even be spiritual.

Physical fatigue is probably healthiest of all since it is produced by exercise and work and it forces rest and facilitates sleep.

Emotional exhaustion is much more difficult to identify and control, and it can be quite complex in its cause. Worry, tension, fear,

---

* (Waco, TX: Word Books, 1986).

and anxiety can be just as exhausting as heavy physical labor, but their impact on our total body system is far more damaging. Excessive noise, conflicts with children or spouse, and even the constant presence of strangers can be quite draining and debilitating.

I am always surprised at how exhausted I feel after entertaining visitors even if they only live with us for a few days. Having to host a dinner function can be as exhausting as running a marathon! "Midnight madness," the inability to get to sleep easily, which often accompanies these emotional stresses, can wreak havoc, especially if you have an active mind.

Spiritual fatigue can follow both physical and emotional exhaustion. In fact, we cannot be spiritually healthy if we neglect physical and emotional healthiness—an important point often overlooked by well-intentioned and highly motivated believers.

The most fatiguing of all vocations that I know of, affecting physical, emotional, and spiritual well-being, is that of being the mother of little children. It is physically demanding, involving constant stooping, lifting, and chasing, as well as many an interrupted night's sleep. The emotions are thrown from one extreme to another, like a piece of driftwood on a stormy sea; it is not uncommon to go from tender love one moment to rage the next. Mothers have to maintain a constant vigil, listening for sounds of trouble even when they are not conscious of it, and they must be ready to leap into action at the slightest hint of something about to be destroyed by tiny hands that have nothing else to do. Exhausting! And then there is little time for spiritual self-nourishment. Add earning a living or being a single parent, and you will be hard-pressed to find a more stressful and fatiguing existence.

One of the worst aspects of fatigue is that it not only depletes the energy needed for happy living, but also distorts perception of the outside world. It makes us angry and irritable, intolerant toward others and incapable of displaying much patience. When we are fatigued, we find it hard to receive love and to care much about loving others.

Yes, fatigue is an enemy to happiness. The remedy lies in finding a way to give the body and mind adequate rest. I hope some of the suggestions in later chapters will help you find emotional and spiritual relief. But unless you resolve to find effective ways to relieve your fatigue of whatever sort, the best advice in all the world will be of little help. Friends, grandparents, a spouse, or even your children may need to be conscripted into your plan for building a happier environment.

A MATTER OF BALANCE

What are the causes of unhappiness? The four factors I have listed here are primary culprits—and there are many other psychological and spiritual causes. But all these causes have one thing in common: The typical unhappy person lives an *unbalanced* life.

A life can be unbalanced in many ways:

- You can desire one thing, pursue one goal, above everything else. For instance, you may want success in your business or profession more than you want it in your marriage. This is unbalanced *desire!*
- You can value one kind of satisfaction over another. It is very easy to prefer certain pleasures (especially the expensive ones) over simple pleasures. This is unbalanced *values!*
- You can place undue emphasis on your need to satisfy your selfish needs. Preoccupation with the self and its needs seldom leads to a happy life. This is unbalanced *emphasis.*
- You can become a devotee of "pleasure," failing to find happiness in the ordinary things of life. You may seek it through intoxication, in whatever form, hoping that oblivion will relieve your monotony. This is unbalanced *devotion.*
- Perhaps the greatest "unbalancing" act of all is to live according to the flesh, neglecting the spirit. When you do this you will always be sabotaging your happiness and disinheriting yourself from the fountainhead of real joy. This is unbalanced *living.*

How then can we restore balance to our distorted lives? Scripture has one very clear prescription, found in Matthew 6:33: "But seek ye first the kingdom of God, and His righteousness; and all these things shall be added unto you."

First things first is a simple but effective rule for complex living. When my wife and I became engaged to be married thirty-six years ago (at a very young age), we had that Scripture engraved on the inside of her engagement ring, and we have tried never to violate its prescription. Our lifelong prayer has been that God would teach us afresh each day how to seek His kingdom first.

Years ago, B. Mansell Ramsey wrote a hymn based on Psalm 25:4–5: "Shew me thy ways, O Lord; Teach me thy paths." The second verse of the hymn sums up how we can live balanced lives in a prayer we could pray often:

When I am sad at heart, Teach me Your way!
When earthly joys depart, Teach me Your way!
In hours of loneliness, in times of dire distress,
In failure or success, Teach me Your way!

This is a prayer that can guarantee happiness under all circumstances—and aim a deadly blow against all the major causes of unhappiness.

CHAPTER THREE

A Biblical View of Happiness

MUCH OF WHAT I HAVE ALREADY WRITTEN HAS, I believe, a sound biblical foundation, and this is no accident. The harmony between God's message to us in Scripture and sound psychological principles of happiness is intentional on God's part. The One who created us knows best what we need for a happy life, and the most expert of psychological investigation into the human condition cannot improve upon His original design.

In this chapter I will add additional thoughts to those already expressed about the biblical perspective on happiness. I believe this is very important, because failure to clarify the biblical boundaries and perspectives can easily cause us to overlook important resources for our own growth.

CAN CHRISTIANS BE HAPPY IN A SUFFERING WORLD?

I actually heard a pastor tell his congregation recently that he didn't believe Christians could ever be happy. He argued that there was so much pain in this world, so much that displeased and saddened God, that no one whose heart is "tuned into" God's could rest peacefully and be happy. Furthermore, he believed that we are actually called to suffer with Christ for the sins of the world and to "pay the price" for the harmful things others were doing to themselves. I was saddened by this message. It contained an element of truth, but it was not helpful to the many who heard him.

Yes, there is a *little* bit of truth to what he said to his very unhappy parishioners. This *is* a sad and broken world we live in. Life is hard for most people. Suffering is rampant, and hunger still ravages billions of the world's people. Even worse, most neglect

God's call to them. It is hard not to be burdened down by the pain of so many hurting people. But we ought not to be surprised by this predicament of human living. Did Jesus not warn us that "in the world [we] shall have tribulation" (John 16:33)? "Tribulation" simply means "trials and sorrows" (LB). And I don't think Jesus was simply warning His disciples that *they* were going to suffer. He was making a statement about the reality of *all* of life: it is full of trouble! This is no less true today than in New Testament times.

But Jesus also said in the *same* verse, "but be of good cheer [or be happy]; I have overcome the world." Amen and Amen!

Let's get another very important point straight: even though this world is now, and will always be, full of suffering and misery, we were not called to suffer in its behalf. It is *not* our role to pay the penalty for the sinful behaviors of God's creatures. That was Christ's purpose in coming into this world. He was the Messiah, and for us to develop a messiah "complex" and think we can help the suffering of others by suffering on their behalf is blatantly ridiculous! Yet there are many who get caught up in this kind of vicarious suffering. The result? They undermine their basis for happiness because they cannot distinguish between God's call to them and the sense of guilt they feel when they see others suffer.

Furthermore, to continue to be unhappy because life is hard for many or because most people choose to ignore God's call in their lives is to ignore Jesus' command to "be of good cheer." Jesus in effect says, "Yes, life is painful; I know this more than anyone. But despite this, I want you to be happy." Only when we obey this command can we be effective in relieving the suffering of others to the best of our ability. Jesus does not call us to "substitutionary suffering," but rather to "substantial service"—service given in His name, in response to His suffering on our behalf. We can find joy (or happiness) in this service.

Can Christians be happy, even though our world is full of suffering? Yes—without question! Perhaps the question is better stated as this: *Should* Christians be happy? I would even dare to go so far as to say that we are *obligated* to rise above our personal pain to demonstrate the transcendent power of an indwelling Christ to a suffering world. If we are believers, we have no choice but to set aside self-pity and self-indulgence and demonstrate to ourselves and others that Jesus has indeed "overcome the world" of our personal tribulations. We *must* seek happiness!

SCRIPTURE PROMISES FOR HAPPINESS

Scripture is full of promises for happiness. Often it uses the word "blessed" because the Greek word *makarios* literally means both "blessed" and "happy." In the Beatitudes, as given in Matthew 5:1–12, the translators of the King James Bible used the old fashioned word *blessed* for "happy." You could just as easily substitute the word *happy* and get a better sense of what Jesus is promising in this important passage.

The word *blessed* does have a very special meaning, however, that I don't want to ignore. It denotes that the happiness God gives is of a very special sort—it is the happiness of His blessings. It is very important that we be happy in the way that God *wants* us to be happy, and that we seek happiness in the places where God wants us to seek it.

For instance, I cannot under any stretch of my imagination believe that anyone can find this kind of happiness through the excessive use of alcohol or any other addictive substance. I have never seen a "blessed" drunk! The "happiness" of alcohol and drugs comes from blotting out the presence of misery, not from the creation of something special. It is lopsided and short-lived— not true happiness of the sort Jesus promised.

Nor can I imagine anyone being deeply happy who pursues happiness only in sex, jogging, eating chocolate, or working long hours at a career. These activities, innocent perhaps in and of themselves, only produce pleasure when they are built upon a more mature foundation of true happiness. They are "icing on the cake," and while they may add a little sparkle to a person's life, they *cannot* be the sum total of all happiness.

Let me illustrate. I love my hobbies. I have lots of them, and I change them as often as the seasons change. I get bored easily, and I love being creative, whether it involves painting in watercolors, building a computer, or repairing a carburetor. I love the sense of accomplishing something, seeing a task completed, or learning some new skill.

There is a danger that I am very aware of, however. If I am not careful, I let the outcome of these leisure pursuits determine my level of happiness. If my watercolor painting turns out to be a blotch, the computer glitches up, or the carburetor disintegrates in the cleaning solvent, I can easily become *very unhappy*. I have to constantly remind myself that these pleasures are only "bonuses" that add sparkle. I must never come to depend on them for my basic happiness.

At bottom line, I must learn to be happy because I am in God's will, doing His bidding, and resting in His grace. *All other things* (including the joy I derive from my family, possessions, friends, and church) merely add enrichment. They must be received thankfully if they bring happiness but not resented if they don't.

HAPPINESS VERSUS JOY

The biblical distinction between happiness and joy is important to recognize. Although the two concepts are related, they are not the same.

The Greek word *chara,* (as in "charismatic") means "joy" or "delight." It is frequently found in the Gospels of Matthew and Luke, and especially in the Gospel of John. For instance, in John 15:11 we read, "These things have I spoken unto you, that my joy might remain in you, and that your joy might be full." This is a definite promise of joy for all believers, and the source of this joy is clearly our life in Christ.

Joy is also presented as one of the "fruits" of the Spirit (Gal. 5:22), together with love, peace, and longsuffering. When Jesus answers prayer, we receive "joy" (John 16:24) and God's kingdom is not made up of what we eat and drink, but of righteousness, peace, and "joy" in the Holy Ghost (Rom. 14:17). These are all wonderful promises of joy for the believer.

Now, as I have said, happiness and joy are not the same. You can be happy (in a superficial sense) but not have joy. You can receive a pay raise, celebrate the occasion with a dinner splurge, or buy a new coat and be happy for a while, but not have the "joy" of which Scripture speaks.

Happiness is more of a "here and now" experience. Often it lasts just for a short time and then vanishes. Joy is presented to us in Scripture as more long-lasting. It has more to do with a state-of-being than with the mood of the moment. Without joy— deep down, God-given, abiding delight in being God's child—it is hard, if not impossible, to build happiness. True happiness, therefore, results from a deeper sense of joy.

The sad thing is that we can have the basic joy of Christian commitment and life in Christ but never translate it into day-to-day, moment-to-moment happiness. The challenge before us always as Christian believers is to let our joy become happiness, every moment of every day, no matter what our circumstances.

TRANSLATING SUFFERING INTO HAPPINESS

An interesting paradox presented in Scripture is that we can be "happy," in the true meaning of the word, even though we are in lhe midst of suffering. First Peter 3:14 points this out clearly: "If ye suffer for righteousness' sake, happy are ye."

How can suffering possibly be of any help in producing happiness? Scripture gives us some very clear explanations for this paradox. Let us take a moment to explore them.

- First of all, we are told that God is to be found in *all* our suffering. He never leaves us to bear it alone. Because of His constant and continuing presence, suffering can be turned to joy. Isaiah knew this when he wrote,

> When thou passest through the waters, I will be with thee; and through the rivers, they shall not overflow thee: when thou walkest through the fire, thou shalt not be burned; neither shall the flame kindle upon thee (Isa. 43:2).

Read Psalm 139 and you will get the same sense of God's ever-present help as the basis for finding joy in your suffering.

- Second, Scripture tells us that suffering (also translated "affliction") can often be a blessing in disguise. Second Corinthians 4:17 makes this point:

> These troubles and sufferings of ours are after all, quite small and won't last very long. Yet this short time of distress will result in God's richest blessing upon us forever and ever! (LB).

During our time of suffering, it seems impossible that any good can come out of our pain. It is only afterwards, when the fire is burnt down or the storm past, when the grass begins to grow again and the birds return to sing, that we see the "peaceable fruit of righteousness" that God has worked (Heb. 12:11). For some, the fruit of their suffering will not be reaped this side of eternity. Not until they have shed their broken body or found final relief for a tortured mind will they see what purpose has been worked through the affliction. Until that moment of relief, they have one purpose to pursue—to find God's joy and express it through their happiness in the here and now. How else can a promise like James 1:2 make sense: "Count it all joy when ye fall into divers temptation"?

- Third, Scripture tells us that suffering of all sorts serves to "purify" our faith. First Peter 1:7 says,

> These trials are only to test your faith, to see whether or not it is strong and pure. It is being tested as fire tests gold and purifies it—and your faith is far more precious to God than mere gold; so if your faith remains strong after being tried in the test tube of fiery trials, it will bring you much praise and glory and honor on the day of his return" (LB).

I often say to my patients, after we have cried together over some painful experience, "God is in the refining business." He is not in the entertainment or pleasure-cruise business. Not that He objects to pleasure cruises or any other diversion that helps us survive our stressful lives. But the purpose of such times of rest and respite is to prepare us for the tough times ahead. They are not an end in themselves. I have never changed a bad habit or strengthened any component of my character while vacationing or having fun. This is not fun's purpose. But it *is* tribulation's purpose.

God wants to build character and endurance. Any marathon runner will tell you that endurance comes from pain—and pushing the boundary of pain further and further back helps to prepare you better for the long haul ahead.

I dabble a little in jewelry making. Having three daughters and a number of secretaries, I need a steady supply of birthday gifts! I enjoy casting rings or broaches in metal and turning lumps of metal into objects of beauty. But success in this process depends on one very important step: how well you "refine" the metal and remove the dirt and dross that will destroy the luster of your creation. Gold may be a precious metal that can be polished to a brilliant shine. But if it is not purged of impurities, it is worthless and never becomes a thing of beauty. So are we in God's sight.

This "refining" process is an exact analogy of the work God does within each of us. The application of heat, purifying chemicals, and patience will produce beauty in any precious metal. Trials, trouble, and suffering received with patience and dedicated to God will build beauty of character and strength for withstanding yet greater trials. This is what Job meant when he wrote, "But he knoweth the way that I take: when he hath tried me, I shall come forth as gold" (Job 23:10).

Who would want to miss the glorious opportunity for God to do this work in you? Afflictions can be God's blessings in disguise because they help achieve a higher purpose. If we *really* believed this, the pain, suffering, and hardship of our lives could be transformed into the stuff happiness is made of. Let's not settle for anything sloppy or sentimental here but find a sense of eternal purpose in *all* of God's work within us.

You may think that this is unworkable, asking too much of ordinary people who must be fathers and mothers, workers and lovers in a world that is imperfect, unfair, and even hostile. Certainly it seems easier—as well as smarter and more sophisticated— to avoid every experience of pain and hardship. But I know of no other way to turn the inevitable experience of pain and suffering of life into real happiness than to dedicate it to God to be used for your own growth and maturation of character.

The less faith you have in God's power to help you transcend your hardships, the less hope you will have of finding the power you need to rise above it. You cannot possibly find happiness in any other way.

PART TWO

15 PRINCIPLES OF HAPPINESS

"Men who are unhappy, like men who sleep badly, are always proud of the fact. Perhaps their pride is like that of the fox who had lost its tail; if so the way to cure it is to point out to them how they can grow a new tail."

Bertrand Russell

"These things have I spoken to you that my joy may be in you and that your joy may be full."

John 15:11

Happiness Is Relative

A FEW YEARS AGO, after many years of absence, my wife and I returned for a visit to the strife-torn land of our birth. We took in our childhood neighborhood, revisited school-day haunts (what was left of them), and reconstructed our courting rendezvous. So much had changed that we felt like strangers in a foreign land. I felt pain everywhere we went, not only because of the political chaos, but also because so many childhood memories were evoked.

While visiting on the outskirts of the town where we had grown up, we went into a small country store to buy a few needed items. As we stopped our borrowed car in front of the store, two small African children approached us. One was a boy of around nine or ten, and the other a girl of eight; they seemed to be brother and sister.

"Please, Master, can you give us twenty-five cents?" begged the boy. I looked at him closely. This was a scene I was very familiar with from my early life in South Africa. Wherever you go in the rural part of the country, there are little boys or girls asking for money. It's just the way things are; the have-nots beg from those who have. South Africans tend to become hardened to it and shoo these unfortunate children away as if they were flies.

But my heart was touched, and I gazed deep into the little boy's eyes. To my surprise, what I saw was a happiness I hadn't seen for a long time in the eyes of American children. This little boy's eyes shone, and his cheeks were deeply dimpled. His face told me that he was happy despite his poverty.

I looked at the little girl, and her face was just as radiant. How is it possible, I wondered, for children with so little in life to be so happy?

"Where is your mother?" I asked the little boy.

"I don't know, Master. We live with an auntie."

31

After some more conversation I discovered that the two of them had been abandoned by their mother, had never known their father, and had no idea where "home" was. They only occasionally went to school. I was totally flabbergasted! Why were their faces full of such obvious happiness? Their smiles reminded me of Proverbs 15:13: "A merry heart maketh a cheerful countenance."

Finally, I asked the little boy, "Why are you so happy?" His reply was simple. "Master, because my stomach is full." Amazing! For him, happiness was simply a matter of having food for the day. I gave him some money and walked away feeling very moved by our encounter—and a little ashamed of the times I have made myself miserable because of a computer glitch or a cancelled appointment.

That little boy's words rang in my mind for many weeks afterwards. He had reminded me of one of the most fundamental happiness principles—that *happiness is relative*. The things that bring happiness to one person don't necessarily bring it to another. For some, just having enough food for that day brings all that is desired. For another who takes having plenty of food for granted, feeling full is not enough.

YOU CAUSE YOUR OWN HAPPINESS

As I have indicated in earlier chapters, happiness depends partly upon your external circumstances but mostly upon what goes on inside you. The person who is unhappy always blames external circumstances. The person who is happy accepts responsibility for these circumstances and sets about to change them.

Certain things are basic, I would think, to our happiness. Mostly they are simple things like food, shelter, health, and love. But even these so-called "essentials" are relative. Take food, for example. For some, a simple meal of porridge and beans would be a sufficient cause for happiness. For others, the largest steak and lobster dinner served in the most elegant restaurant wouldn't do it. Happiness is relative!

Take shelter as another example. For some, anything that stops the wind from howling round their ears and keeps the frost off their faces would be sufficient for happiness. For others, a mansion with high ceilings and ornate banisters would not be a sufficient abode.

We have recently been confronted with the plight of the homeless in many of our cities. People who want to work but can't earn enough to pay for shelter; families who try to stay together by living out of their automobiles or in abandoned buildings and who spend every third or fourth night in a motel just so they can wash. Ask one of these unfortunates: "What would make you happy?" I think you would be surprised by how little it would take to satisfy their needs. It's all relative, you see.

One very important key to being happy, therefore, is to make sure you do not lose your perspective on what you've got nor exaggerate what you need. Happy people are those who can live with *perspective*, constantly striving to balance the ratio of what they have to what they want. If you often want more than you have, you are in unhappy territory.

VALUE WHAT YOU ALREADY HAVE

A major cause of unhappiness is *not valuing what we already have*. It is in our nature quickly to become dissatisfied with what we've got. I suspect this tendency is a residual component of our sinful nature! I notice it strongly in myself and must constantly look out for it.

For example, I love having different types of wristwatches. I like them to have lots of gadgets. When wristwatches first came out with built-in alarms (long before digital watches), I was ecstatic. I could set the alarm to wake me up, to tell me when I had preached long enough, or to remind me of an appointment.

Then waterproof watches came out, and I was unhappy with my alarm wristwatch. I decided it was inconvenient and even time-consuming to have to take off a watch when I showered. So I bought a waterproof watch, thinking it would make me happy, but forgetting the principle that happiness is always relative!

A few months later, the mail-order catalog announced a new watch—one that combined an alarm with a waterproof case. Once again I was dissatisfied; I had to have this watch also. Soon after, digital watches were invented. I found myself needing one that could beep me every hour, *and* perform as a stopwatch, *and* be submersible. Then there appeared a watch with a calculator that could preserve my bank balance, as well as one that could measure temperature and remember telephone numbers. My latest watch measures my heartrate, beat by beat.

Whenever will they stop enticing me by inventing new wristwatches? Even my wife is becoming hooked. She showed me an advertisement the other day for a virtual wrist-sized computer!

I reminded her that I was trying hard to put into practice what I preach: happiness is being able to value *what you already have.*

Do you get my point? To be happy we must constantly put all our desires in proper perspective and find contentment in what we have and where we are. This is the message of Paul in Philippians 4:11: "I have learned, in whatsoever state I am, therewith to be content." In other words, value what you've got. Don't expect to find happiness in that next watch!

HAPPINESS IS LIVING OBJECTIVELY

Another cause of unhappiness is *wanting more than you can reasonably expect.*

I suppose that if you are in prison it is natural for you to be unhappy. It is normal under this circumstance to want freedom and to expect that your freedom will bring a measure of happiness. This is a reasonable expectation.

But most of us are not realistic in what we expect from life. I am not alluding to envy here, nor to a tendency to have unreasonable expectations in everyday matters. These I will discuss in a later chapter. No, I am referring to the chip most of us carry on our shoulders because we want more than we have. We are angry at life, our parents, or God for not giving us prettier faces, stronger bodies, or brighter minds. We bemoan the fact that we haven't had better opportunities or lived in a world ready to receive and affirm us. Perhaps we have even started life with all the cards stacked against us because of poverty, unsatisfactory parents, or a debilitating handicap. No matter! We must live with objectivity on what we are or have. And when we lack this ability to put all our shortcomings or lack of assets in objective perspective, we quickly become unhappy.

Allow me to illustrate this point briefly. In my mid-twenties, when I still worked as a civil engineer, I became quite friendly with a fellow engineer. He was a bit older, probably in his late forties, and unmarried. This surprised me at first because he was quite handsome, successful in his profession, and seemingly a pleasant person. But as I got to know him better, I learned that he was a deeply troubled man. I even heard rumors that he had attempted suicide several times.

I had little or no clinical expertise at that stage in my life, so I could not offer this man any therapeutic help. I did, however, share my personal testimony with him, in the hope that he would respond with a desire to receive Christ into his life.

At first he was quite hostile to my conversations and made it clear that he didn't believe there was a God. His deep bitterness toward life (which he had brought on himself) was quite evident. I tried to point him to God's perspective on our physical existence, but to no avail. Finally he told me something about himself. His parents had abandoned him as a baby, and he had grown up in an orphanage. All his life he had felt that no one cared about him. His singleness was a source of deep resentment; he deeply wanted a mutually satisfying relationship with a woman, but could not allow anyone to "get close" for fear he would once again be abandoned.

Shortly after we began our talks, I received a telephone call from a fellow worker one Saturday morning. My friend had once again attempted suicide—and this time he had succeeded. His death saddened me deeply, because this man had brought most of his misery on himself. True, he had suffered as a child. But much of his unhappiness grew out of his inability to look at his life objectively, to appreciate what he had going for him, to deal with his resentments, and form close attachments. I promised God and myself that I would never let my life get that far out of perspective.

WHERE DO WE NEED OBJECTIVITY?

Because the things that cause happiness are so relative, one thing being enough for one person and not enough for another, we need to inject a great deal of objectivity into the way we view our world. Remind yourself often that true happiness does not consist in having, but in being. It is not in possessing that we find happiness, but in knowing how to enjoy what we already have. No matter how disadvantaged you feel up to this point in your life, you can begin to change the future.

In what areas of our lives do we really need this objectivity? Let me suggest a few:

Materialism

We need objectivity in our quest to acquire material possessions about as much as we need it anywhere. Our western world is materialistically minded. We are told in many subtle ways (and some not-so-subtle) that the more we possess the happier we will be—and that it is God's will that we all have as much as we desire. "God never wants us to fail. His will is that we always succeed," I heard a prominent TV preacher tell the world this past Sunday. Unfortunately this view feeds our materialistic desires, and it has rubbed off on all of us. It permeates our churches and our Christian faith, and we don't even recognize it. It is the cause of much unhappiness.

A brilliant young business executive sat in my office the other day. With tears streaming down his face, he said, "My father promised me that when I had made my first million I would be a very happy person. He lied! He told me that just to force me to be successful."

Sad, isn't it? Money and success do not bring happiness *unless* one knows how to use these things in meaningful ways. In fact, I don't think you can be happy as a rich person unless you can also be happy with nothing.

Now, I have nothing against becoming rich. In fact, to be honest, I'd like to give it a try sometime! Wealth, in itself, is neutral; it neither gives happiness nor takes it away. It is what we *do* with our wealth—and how objective we are in having or not having it —that determines our happiness.

To keep your materialism in proper perspective, I would suggest you regularly ask yourself the following questions, especially when considering a major material acquisition:

- Do I *really need* this thing I want?
- Am I making the best use of what I already have?
- Should I remember the needs of others before fulfilling my own "needs"?
- What would Jesus do if He were in my shoes right now?

If you attempt to answer these questions honestly, you will be taking giant strides toward a more objective lifestyle.

Sexuality

We also need objectivity in our quest for sexual satisfaction. I have long believed that our society is sexually neurotic. By this I mean that we are so sexually inhibited on the one hand, yet so obsessed by sex on the other, that we distort this beautiful gift of God to the point that this distortion can destroy our happiness. We've lost our objectivity to such an extent that a great many people are searching for an extraordinary experience or a novel sexual adventure that doesn't exist and would not bring them happiness even if it did!

Why do many men, especially when they get to the so-called

"midlife" phase, desire an illicit sexual encounter? (If they don't outwardly seek it, they certainly fantasize about it.) Is this merely an attempt to recapture their virile youthfulness? I doubt it. I think it is more a matter of their losing objectivity and somehow coming to believe that a new sexual experience or a new partner will solve all their unhappiness problems. Furthermore, because they haven't mastered the art of being happy at a fundamental level, they seek happiness even more in sexual thrills. I believe this strongly because I have never known a man (or a woman for that matter) who has mastered the basic happiness-building skills I am discussing in this book and yet has run away with someone else during a midlife period. It is *unhappy people* (Christian believers included) who are at risk for extramarital affairs!

One last thought on sexuality as it relates to living objectively: Sexuality tends to be very selfish in our culture. We believe that satisfaction comes from receiving, rather than from giving, pleasure. We want to receive love more than we want to give it. We are encouraged to focus on our personal satisfactions, not on our responsibility to see that others are also satisfied. Such self-centeredness never produces lasting happiness.

The Opinions of Others

Have you ever pondered the life of Jesus from the perspective of happiness? Have you considered that His happiness and the fulfillment of His life's purpose did not depend on the things we so desperately cling to and define as essential to our happiness? Listen to what was written about Him: "He was in the world, and the world was made by him, and the world knew him not. He came unto his own, and his own received him not" (John 1:10–11).

Very few people can be happy unless they are being approved by those around them. The need for social approval—the applause and affirmation of others—and the fear of rejection are both strong forces in our lives which move us toward or away from happiness. From our earliest years, we learn to do those things that please others. First we want to please our parents, then our brothers and sisters, and later our friends. God might just get His turn if we live long enough!

What's wrong with this? Don't we all need affirmation? Don't we have a need to know whether we're doing a good job or not? Isn't this just plainly and simply a fact of life?

Very true. The problem, however, is that the approval of others, as with so many other things, is very relative. We may get approval one day for doing something, then be rejected the next day for doing the very same thing—it all depends on the mood of those who do the approving. Parents are as guilty as siblings or friends. They may change their expectations of us without giving us adequate notice, so that what pleases them today will shift to something else tomorrow.

Furthermore, it is a plain fact that people differ among themselves as to what should be applauded and what rejected. The old saying is still true: *You just can't please everyone!*

Try standing up in a public church meeting and stating your opinion on some matter. Will everyone agree with you? I doubt it! We are all made to be different, so how can we expect everyone to agree on anything? Great men and women over the centuries have disagreed even about the most important issue of all: Who is God? I certainly don't expect to get everyone's agreement on such an issue, even though I know Him personally. So how can I expect to have everyone agree on lesser issues?

If you have strong convictions, you are bound to be rejected by some other people, if not all of them, and a great deal of unhappiness will result if you don't watch your reactions. Chances are that a few will isolate you and even make your surroundings hostile.

This is what happened to Jesus, and if He had not kept His rejection in proper perspective, seeing the approval of the populace as a relative thing, as changeable as the wind, He could not have stayed true to God's plan for His life.

If you are waiting for sympathetic surroundings before you can be happy, you have a long wait ahead. If you cannot be happy unless you feel that others approve your values or behavior, you'll never be happy. If your happiness depends on doing only what others want you to do, you will stunt your growth toward spiritual and psychological maturity, and you will live in constant fear of rejection.

Jesus did not fear public opinion. He never let the opinions of others change His attitudes or actions, and He made no attempt to "create the right impression" just so people would follow Him. He did His work faithfully and obediently, free of the tyranny of "what will others think?"

You and I *can also live this way* because He can empower us. The more we do so, the happier we will be.

HELPFUL THOUGHTS

Since happiness is relative and a matter of perspective, focus your thinking and praying on the following perspective-building exercises. I suggest you take one for each day of the week and seek to apply its principle to every aspect of your life during that day.

- Write down five accomplishments or goals you desire to achieve in your life. Alongside each, give at least one reason why it's absolutely *not* necessary for you to get what you want.
- Identify five objects you already own—a car, stereo, boat, or whatever. Pray over each one of these things, asking God to help you value them more or to help you get rid of them if they are cluttering your life.
- List five people you care for very much. Beside each person's name, write down something positive you would want that person to have or to be able to do. Pray that each will get what you want for him or her.
- Think of some person you might have hurt or harmed. Pray for this person's healing and for the restoration of a happy relationship.
- Write down five disappointments or losses you have experienced in your life. Pray about each one of them, asking God to show you whether or not you should still think of it as a disappointment or loss.
- Identify two or three people whose opinions you value and who have power to approve or disapprove of you. Think of some ways in which you can reduce this power without upsetting the relationship.
- Name five things God has done for you. Pray about each one of them, thanking Him for His bountiful gifts and asking for forgiveness if you have not been thankful.

PRINCIPLE TWO

Happiness Is a Choice

ONE BEAUTIFUL SUNNY DAY, a visitor from the city was walking down a country road when he saw a farmer leaning against the fence in front of his barn. Thinking he would display his city friendliness, he walked over to the farmer and said, "Nice day, isn't it? Must be good for the corn!"

"Yes," replied the farmer, "but it's bad for the potatoes." Nothing more was said.

The following day was dark with thick, threatening clouds overhead. The friendly visitor again walked over to the farmer and said, "Nice day, isn't it? Must be good for the potatoes."

"Yes," replied the farmer, "but it's bad for the corn!"

This is a common predicament. Some days are good for corn, while others are good for potatoes. And many people go through life unhappy because they can't choose which they prefer!

All of life has at least two sides—the sunny side, which is good for some things but bad for others, and the cloudy side. If you are not careful about your attitude, you will lose *both ways*, because you will never discover which side of life is best for you. Sunny or cloudy, corn or potatoes, happiness is a *choice*. You have to *choose* to be happy, no matter what your circumstances. If you fail to do so, unhappiness will automatically take over.

This is one of the simplest yet most liberating principles I know. Others don't determine whether I am happy or not. I do. Circumstances don't control my happiness. I do. And the point of control lies in my ability to *choose* which set of circumstances I will allow to *define* my happiness.

HAPPINESS IS A CHOICE—WITH PEOPLE

People—especially friends or family—are a major cause of happiness or unhappiness. I suppose this is to be expected. Only

41

people react to us. Only people take revenge—not animals or cars. Only people remember hurts and store up resentment—not books or trees! So the primary area where we must exercise the principle of "choosing our happiness" is in our relationships.

A very common belief many of us hold is that the actions of *others* determine our happiness level. "If he only loved me more, I would be happy." Or, "If she only would initiate love and take the first step, I would be happy."

The other day I actually heard a husband say, "If only my wife would open the garage door for me just before I arrived home from work, I'd know she loved me." I couldn't believe what I was hearing! True, this man hated getting out of the car to open the door. But it seemed to me that if what he was saying was true, an electric door-opener could easily replace the wife he said he loved!

I challenged him. "If only . . . ?" I asked. The idea was obviously ridiculous. If his wife did open the door regularly for him, he'd invent something else she would have to do to make him happy. My friend must learn to choose his happiness no matter what his wife does not do.

The point I am making here is that we cannot control what others *do* or *don't* do to or for us. Everything is a gift, especially love.

We also cannot control what people *say*. I had a client once whose husband was rather brutal with his tongue. Over weekends, especially, he would verbally attack her, saying things like "You're as stupid as your mother," or "You're so useless, I don't know why your father didn't give you up for adoption when you were born." This woman was determined not to break up the marriage, but she felt beaten down by such verbal abuse. Even though I pleaded with the husband to control his tongue (he denied meaning what he said), the attacks continued unabated, so I had to help the wife cope with this unhappy situation.

My approach was simple. "Words don't have to hurt," I told her. "After all, they are only symbols. You can *choose* whether you want them to hurt you or not. Do you remember the rhyme you used to say when you were a child: 'Sticks and stones may break my bones, but words can never hurt me'?"

What great words of wisdom are in this child's rhyme. My mother checked my anger and desire for revenge against my younger brother's taunts many times with these words. And now I was helping a verbally abused wife to ward off the vicious taunts of a disturbed husband by reminding her that words are only symbols; they don't hurt unless we allow them to. That's as true for grownups as it is for children.

In healthier relationships, one can usually address the problem of what people say by opening up better communication and direct confrontation of hurtful actions. But this marriage was far beyond any normal intervention and needed a period of "cooling off" before more effective therapy could be introduced. Until an alternative course of action can be taken, all a hurting person can do is *choose* not to interpret words at face value. If you cannot get away from them, shut them off at your ears!

The same applies to what others *think*. You cannot control what people think about you. You can only control how you react to those other people's opinions.

Surely you are like me! Every now and then I get caught up in worrying about what others are thinking. "Why does Bill look at me that way?" "Does she respect what I am doing?" "How will this action of mine come across to him?" Thoughts like these flash across my mind a thousand times when I am preoccupied with the opinions of others.

Psychologist Will Snyder calls this "impression monitoring," a phenomenon I'll say more about later. This means you constantly check up on the *impression* you are making on others. The more hung-up you are on what others think about you, the more inhibited you become, and the less likely you are to have the freedom to be yourself. Consequence? You will be unhappy.

Since you cannot control what others think about you, your only healthy alternative is to *choose* not to be bothered by it.

Please understand what I am saying. I am not advocating an attitude of "I don't care what anyone says or thinks." I am not encouraging an extreme disregard for the opinions of others—such an attitude would clearly be pathological. But I am encouraging you not to be preoccupied with and overly sensitive to what you think others are thinking. Don't let what others do, say, or think determine your happiness. If you do, you literally give other people control over your life, and happiness goes out the window.

HAPPINESS IS A CHOICE—WITH CIRCUMSTANCES

There are many things that happen to us in life over which we have no control. We recently experienced a fairly large earthquake in Los Angeles. It came unexpectedly, even though "earthquake preparedness" is a big emphasis in California. I was driving to work just before eight in the morning when the earthquake hit. It felt as if all four tires had blown out, with the car swaying side to side. I stopped the car to inspect the tires, only to find that other drivers were doing the same. Then I saw the trees swaying and felt the earth rolling. Immediately I turned the car around and headed home to be with my family.

As I was driving back to my home, I realized again how little control we have over much that happens to us. One moment I was peaceably driving to work, anticipating an ordinary day, and the next I was caught up in what could possibly be a disaster for all of my family. How thankful I was that God was in control of our lives! Fortunately, I discovered that no harm had been done at my home. A friend of mine, who lives right over the earthquake's epicenter, was not so fortunate—half his home was demolished!

How are we to handle the uncertainties of life? How do we cope with unpredictability? If we worry about "what could happen," we might all become ill. But if we ignore the possibility of unforeseen circumstances, we might not be sufficiently prepared to survive them—Scripture tells us not to be too confident about the future because we don't know "what a day may bring forth" (Prov. 27:1).

Between these extremes we have to live a happy life. How do we do it? By choosing to live in harmony with the circumstances over which we have no control! This, in the final analysis, is a matter of faith.

Of course, some circumstances that cause unhappiness *are* controllable. If we drive on well-worn tires and have a blowout on a busy highway at high speed, we have *chosen* that circumstance. If we neglect to build relationships and end up lonely and disliked, we have *chosen* this circumstance. If we neglect our spiritual growth by failing to develop a disciplined prayer life and then find our lives to be barren and hollow, we have *chosen* this circumstance. Neglecting *is* choosing. Unfortunately, it may mean choosing the wrong thing.

In emphasizing that we have the freedom to choose our happiness in circumstances we can control as well as in those we cannot control, I am trying to shift the responsibility for our happiness back where it belongs—on ourselves. It is very easy to blame our unhappiness on other people or uncontrollable circumstances and therefore not to take responsibility for it. And it's easy to fall into a fatalistic attitude of "If it's going to happen, it's going to happen, and there's nothing I can do about it." The trouble is, such an attitude will not help us be happier; in fact, it almost guarantees our unhappiness!

The alternative is to live responsibly—reacting maturely to every circumstance and looking at adversity as a challenge to make things better. If we do this, we will always be happy—even if we don't succeed in everything we do.

DEFINING YOUR HAPPINESS

Choosing to be happy requires that attention be given to a further mental phenomenon. I call it "defining your happiness." Actually, it works both ways; we can either define our happiness or define our *un*happiness.

This is how it works. When I say to myself, "I will never be happy until I have a thousand dollars in the bank," I am "defining" my happiness. I am stating the condition that must be met for me to be happy. Perhaps a thousand dollars in the bank is achievable, perhaps it isn't. If it is, then my happiness is guaranteed. If it isn't, I am creating my own unhappiness.

If I were to say, "I will never be happy until I have traveled at least once around the world," I may be defining a condition for my happiness that is beyond reasonable attainment. Consequently, I will be *choosing* to be unhappy.

Defining our unhappiness works in a similar way. I can say to myself, "Unless I am chosen to represent my school on the swim team, I will be unhappy." Each time we do something like this, we set up our unhappiness by defining its conditions.

We do define our happiness or unhappiness all the time without realizing it. For instance, I have a friend who convinced himself that unless he had achieved success by the age of forty-five, he would consider himself to be a failure. He "defined" success as reaching a certain level of seniority in the company for which he worked. As my friend approached his forty-fifth birthday (without having obtained the desired level of seniority), he became deeply depressed. He had created his unhappiness by arbitrarily defining age forty-five as the age at which he must have arrived at glory and honor—plus arbitrarily designating a certain position as representing success.

I reasoned with him: "What law says that age forty-five is the magic age? And who says that such and such a position in your company is equal to being a success?" I explained that he was *defining* his happiness in a way that would almost certainly guarantee his unhappiness. Slowly, then, my friend began the process of "unde-fining" the conditions he had set for his happiness.

Why don't you take a moment to examine the ways you tend to define your happiness or unhappiness? Here are some examples of "defining" statements I have often heard that may sound familiar to you:

- "If it is sunny on Saturday so I can go to the beach and sunbathe, then I'll be happy." (It may rain all weekend, so why not make alternative plans for something you can do indoors as well?)
- "If my husband says I cooked a great meal this evening, then I'll be happy." (Fat chance of this happening! Why not just make your meal an "unconditional" gift to your husband?)
- "If I win the lottery, then I'll be happy." (So will millions of others who also think they will win! Be content to work for your wealth.)
- And on and on and on. . . .

So often, we define our happiness according to insignificant and unimportant conditions. And simply by setting up those conditions, we tend to create the possibility of unhappiness. Could we not just as easily choose to be happy without stipulating a condition? Or, better still, could we plan on being happy no matter what the conditions are?

Of course we can! We can define our happiness in more positive ways and thus choose to be happy more often. We could say things like:

- "Because God loves me, I'm going to be happy today."
- "If I can do one deed of love to a stranger today, I'll be happy."
- "If I have friends and family to thank God for, I'll be happy."

There's nothing wrong with defining the conditions of our happiness, as long as they are reasonable and in keeping with God's plan for our lives.

Choosing to be happy is not difficult. Often, as I drive to work in the morning, I consciously and deliberately say to myself, "Today, I will be happy no matter what awaits me." Simply affirming a statement like this at the beginning of the day helps me form a right attitude and shapes my mood. You can do the same.

HELPFUL THOUGHTS

To help you choose your happiness, let me suggest a few self-affirmations. You may wish to write each of them on a three-by-five card. Then you can carry the cards with you wherever you go or place them in strategic places where they can remind you to exercise your freedom to "choose."

- *Just for today* I will set my affection on things above, not on things on the earth.
- *Just for today* I will not worry about what will happen tomorrow, but will trust that God will go before me into the unknown.
- *Just for today* I will endure anything that hurts or depresses me because I believe God controls what happens to me.
- *Just for today* I will not dwell on my misfortunes. I will replace my negative thoughts with happy and hopeful thoughts.
- *Just for today* I will choose to do some things I do not like doing, and I will do them cheerfully and with a happy spirit.
- *Just for today* I will make a conscious effort to love those who don't show love to me and be kind to those who do not appreciate me.
- *Just for today* I will be patient with those who irritate me and longsuffering toward those who are selfish and inconsiderate.
- *Just for today* I will be courageous. I will take responsibility for all my actions and not blame others for the way I behave.
- *Just for today* I will not demand more of myself than I do from others nor condemn myself because I don't measure up to my unreasonable expectations.
- *Just for today* I will forgive all those who hurt me—even forgiving myself.
- *Just for today* I will choose to BE HAPPY!

Happiness Is Getting Your Eyes Off Others

THERE WAS A TIME, when I was in my early twenties and working at my first "real" job, that I desperately wanted to buy my own car. But I simply didn't have the funds; I had to make do with an old bicycle someone had loaned me.

And then one day another newly qualified engineer came to work in a brand new MG sports car. It was the older style "TD" that was popular all over the world in its day (the mid-fifties) and is now a classic.

I became very unhappy. That young man's parents were wealthy and could give him a car as a graduation present. And I couldn't even buy my own bicycle!

I remember my self-talk. It included such questions as "Why do others have everything?" "Why must I always be the one to wait?" "When will I ever get a turn at the good things of life?" My misery lasted many months as I observed my friend lovingly polishing the chrome or breezing down the street in that beautiful car. And I remained unhappy until finally I was able to buy my first car, a ten-year-old, beat-up Austin.

After we married, Kathleen and I bought a piece of land and built our first home. I planned it, engaged subcontractors, and built much of it myself, laboring over cupboards and painting with much satisfaction. Finally it was completed, and we moved in.

And then another engineer friend built himself a home—a bigger, fancier home—in the lot right behind ours. And instead of enjoying to the fullest the home I had built, I became unhappy. I envied what my friend had accomplished.

Slowly a truth dawned on me: I will never be happy unless I get my eyes off what other people accomplish or possess. It was true for the car my friend got, as well as for the home my other friend built.

Dr. Allen Parducci, a prominent UCLA researcher who

specializes in the study of happiness, reports that money, success, health, beauty, intelligence, or power do not necessarily produce a happy life. Instead, the level of a person's happiness is determined largely by whether that person compares himself or herself with other people whose circumstances are better or worse than their own.*

Now, when I see someone else get a promotion, buy a new and bigger car, achieve success with a book, or take exotic vacations, I try to remind myself, "Be thankful for what you've got! Don't compare yourself with others. They are entitled to be successful also!" After many years of saying this to myself, I am at last beginning to believe it—and I am a much happier person!

Hebrews 13:5 must surely be as hard to obey as any scripture: "Let your conversation be without covetousness; and be content with such things as ye have; for he hath said, I will never leave thee, nor forsake thee." But to gain happiness you must learn to enjoy what you've got. In building a happy and contented life, you must appreciate your present blessings, not envy what you don't have. And the bonus is that God promises never to leave us! No matter what others receive—even if what they receive is better than what you have—God's blessings will always make up the difference.

ENVY CAUSES UNHAPPINESS

Envy is, next to worry, one of the most potent causes of unhappiness. Watching what others receive and keeping score of their successes tends to destroy appreciation for our own gifts and successes. Envy distorts our vision, making us unable to see things for their own value, but only for their value in comparison with others.

And envy is in all of us, make no mistake. If you say otherwise, either you don't know yourself well or you just haven't labelled your feelings correctly. Envy is a universal emotion. It is present in little children, as my grandchildren remind me daily. If Vincent (the older grandson) receives a gift, Allen (the younger) wants it also. And always having to give the same gift to both of them gets expensive!

By the time Vincent was three-and-a-half years old, he had learned that if his younger brother didn't get exactly the same gift

---

* *Star News*, 30 January 1983.

as he did, he ran the risk of having to give it up to Allen during a temper tantrum. So he would always ask, "But what about Allen? Doesn't he get the same also?" By insisting that they both get similar gifts, Vincent was able to keep Allen's envy to a minimum and thus ensure that they were both happy. Smart boy! But life isn't always that cooperative, and someone else always ends up with more!

Happy people are able to accept the "give and take" of life. At one moment they may have the advantage, but the next someone else may have it. This year they may get a promotion, but next year someone else may get one. To be happy, you must be able to rejoice in both these circumstances—in your own promotion and in the promotion of someone else. Everyone ought to have a turn at the good things of life. You cannot have it all for yourself—unless you want to be very unhappy.

Happy people are also able to let other people be better than they are. Here I am touching on a very personal "sore point," because I tend to be very competitive when it comes to comparing competence. I have always wanted to be the best at anything I do. This would be quite healthy, except that I translate it into meaning, "I want to be *better* than anyone else."

As a young engineer, I wanted to be the quickest, smartest, most creative engineer in the office. Perhaps I succeeded a little, because I won promotions very quickly. But whenever I encountered a competitor who was quicker, smarter, and more creative, I became extremely unhappy—and my resentment showed!

It took much patience on God's part finally to bring me to the place of maturity where I could free others to be better than I am. This does not diminish my level of competence; it simply acknowledges that God has given us (with a little help from our parent's genes) varying levels of skill and brilliance. I am happiest when I fulfill *my* level of competence, and leave others to fulfill theirs.

THE PERILS OF ENVY

Why is envy so perilous?

First, *envy distorts our ability to be grateful.* We cannot be thankful for what we have if we are envious of what others have. When anything pleasant happens, we need to be able to enjoy it to the fullest without wondering whether someone else has had a better experience.

Envy is fatal to happiness! It poisons the spirit of gratitude. The envious person says, "Yes, I have a secure job, good friends, and a lovely home, but I believe that people in Timbuktu have it better. They don't work half as hard as I do to get the same things." And as he thinks this, his job becomes less satisfying, his friends less desirable, and his home more like a hovel. Comparisons are pointless and foolish; they only result in unhappiness.

Second, *envy diminishes our love for others*. If we envy someone else's belongings, we will resent that person, too. Love cannot peacefully coexist with feelings of envy. Our eyes keep drifting to the advantage the other person has over us, and we cannot love freely.

Third, *envy disrupts peace*. Discontent, dissatisfaction, and heightened frustration will follow envy and become a part of our characters. We may even wish misfortune on those we envy, only to find our ill wishes boomerang on us. Many wars have been started by people who want something that someone else has.

Fourth, *envy misdirects our competitiveness*, making us strive to gain from others the things we envy. This is a major obstacle to happiness. Wanting to be as attractive or popular as our friends can set us up to be in competition with them and thus destroy the friendship. Even the pursuit of excellence in a given pursuit can become a passion to gain something we envy in another person rather than a drive to fulfill our own potential. Unchecked, this kind of competitiveness can ruin any hope of deep inner joy.

Finally, envy *grieves* God because it reveals a lack of appreciation for all His love and care. Every parent of teenagers knows what it feels like when a child goes through that difficult stage of knowing everything, wanting everything, and appreciating nothing. Surely our heavenly Father feels the same kind of grief over His children who spoil their own and others' happiness by a spirit of envy!

THE CURE FOR ENVY

What is the cure for envy? I only know of one really effective cure: a deep spiritual renewal that makes us so thankful for what God has done for us that the advantages others may have pale into insignificance. To focus on God's gifts to us without wanting what others have can free us to enjoy what we've got without robbing those others of what they are entitled to.

Having first of all established a spiritual basis for coping with envy, I can make a few other practical suggestions to help you overcome this happiness-killer.

- Begin by placing a greater emphasis on the value of selflessness in your life. Think and pray about the Christlikeness you would like to show others.
- Since an unhappy childhood may be a major factor in promoting envy, you may want to reevaluate your early life experiences. (If necessary, seek the help of a professional counselor to help you do this.) You may have to dispense large doses of forgiveness in order to be done with any residual resentments that could be fostering envy.
- Break the habit of thinking in comparisons. When someone else experiences something pleasant, enter into the joy of the occasion. Make a telephone call or write a letter and "rejoice with them that rejoice."
- Develop the habit of thankfulness. Be thankful for *every* blessing, no matter how small. Never let a disappointment occur without finding some aspect of it to rejoice over.
- Every time you feel a spirit of envy overcoming you, give it over to God in prayer. Confess it as a sin and seek forgiveness for it. This is a discipline that will eradicate even the deepest envy.

Believers beware! It is possible to become envious even of the spiritual gifts of others and to destroy your happiness in the envious pursuit of the power you see in others. Temptation is always subtle, and envy can invade our quest to be better Christians just as easily as it can spoil our other ambitions. We need all the wisdom God can give us when it comes to dealing with our spiritual envies!

THE PERILS OF AFFIRMATION

"Keeping your eyes off others" involves more than avoiding envy. It also involves the way we look to other people for approval or affirmation.

We all need a certain amount of approval in order to be happy. It would be ridiculous to suggest that we can live indifferently to whether or not we are loved or doing a good job. We want to be appreciated and to know we have a place in this world.

The problem, of course, is that we do not always receive such affirmation in our lives. Therefore, unless we can build some freedom from dependence on this appreciation we will not achieve our fullest happiness. Clearly, it should be every believer's goal to become much more dependent on God's affirmation—and much less concerned about whether our spouse, father, pastor, friends, or neighbors are appreciating us. If we can achieve this, we may be pleasantly surprised how much affirmation we do receive. The problem is mainly our preoccupation with this need, and when we reduce this preoccupation, we achieve a freedom to be more loving and spontaneous—and others respond to us more positively.

Scripture affirms many times that our primary focus must be on receiving God's approval—not the approval of other people. In the parable of the talents (Matt. 25), the Lord says to the profitable servant, who had concentrated on pleasing the master and no one else, "Well done, good and faithful servant; thou has been faithful over a few things; I will make thee ruler over many things: enter thou into the joy of thy Lord" (v. 23).

Again in Hebrews 11 and 12, where we are presented with the long list of God's faithful servants, we are told to "lay aside every weight . . . run with patience the race that is set before us, looking unto Jesus the author and finisher of our faith" (Heb. 12:1-2).

Get your eyes off others; keep them off others; focus them on God's provisions for you and on His approval, and you will be laying a solid foundation for your happiness.

THE PERILS OF SELF-PITY

Life is a mixed bag of joy and sadness, pain and growth. Happy people are able to accept the whole package of life without trying to fish out only the good parts.

When I was a little boy my mother made "tickey pudding" at Christmas time. It was a special Christmas pudding made with dried fruit, plums, nuts, and cherries, and into the soft mix, before it was baked, she would stir in a handful of small silver English coins called "tickeys." (I still have a few I've kept in my coin box as mementos. They still have pieces of pudding stuck to them!) On Christmas day the pudding was served last, piping hot, with lots of custard over the top.

Actually, my younger brother and I never really liked the pudding. But we loved finding tickeys! We pleaded for large helpings, dug through the pudding with our spoons searching for the coins, and discarded the nuts, raisins and cherries as not worthy of our discriminating palates. But Mother's voice would rise above the hubbub of the large family gathering: "Kids, you eat it all, or you don't get the tickeys!" What a disappointment! She had this principle we could never quite understand, which said "You eat it all, or you take nothing." It goes together as one package, she insisted—good and bad, the pudding with the coins.

Life is like that. Take it all, or you take nothing. The bad goes with the good, and vice-versa! You can't be selective. Old age goes with youth, wealth with poverty, and sickness with health. We can't dig through life looking only for its rewards and discarding the real stuff of which life is made.

It is very easy not to understand this and therefore give way to self-pity and deep dissatisfaction, because life always has some unpleasantness to serve alongside the pleasant. We then look to others for sympathy. But while there are a few saints who know how to give sympathy in the right way, I doubt if there are many. Most people either sympathize in a way that makes us pity ourselves even more, or they become as emotionally involved as we are and lose their objectivity and ability to guide us back to accepting "the whole package."

God is the source of all mercy and "the God of all comfort" (2 Cor. 1:3). He comforts better than any mother (Isa. 66:13) and is always available to us. Therefore the happy person, instead of wasting time on self-pity or fruitlessly looking for comfort, goes directly to the Source of all comfort.

HELPFUL THOUGHTS

To help you "get your eyes off others," here are some thoughts you can focus on through each day:

- The fact that some people may possess superior skills in one way or another does not make them superior to me as a human being.
- Everyone has faults, limitations, and insecurities as well as assets. I must not exaggerate nor diminish the value of others in my own eyes.
- Most people do not like me to compete with them. If anything, they want to feel equal to me, not inferior.

- Notions of superiority or inferiority are very dangerous to myself and others. I must try my best not to compare myself with others.
- It is just as dangerous to think I am superior as it is to think I am inferior. Superiority breeds arrogance and leads to the abuse of power.
- Instead of being competitive, I can look for intrinsic good qualities in others (like kindness, compassion or humor). God creates us all equal.

Happiness Is Being Able to Forgive

I GREW UP in a little town in South Africa where almost everyone was connected in some way with gold mining. The mines dominated our landscape, and they provided all the recreational facilities for us kids. We played our games on the mine "dumps"— clambering all over those mountains of stone that had been blasted out of the rock five thousand feet underground and hauled to the surface so the gold could be extracted.

After a week of playing on the dumps, we found it difficult to settle down for an hour of Sunday school. But we went anyway, to the tiny Methodist church our English-speaking community had built some years before I was born. It was just expected of us all!

I can clearly remember my feelings about Sunday school—a mixture of resentment at being required to dress up and forego my games, along with a deep satisfaction with the way our teachers, two devout older ladies, presented the claims of the gospel to us. One of our teachers was a former Salvation Army officer, the mother of one of my best friends. And the other, a special friend of mine, was known to us simply as "Auntie Jo."

Auntie Jo was always kind, and she was full of love and respect for all the kids. She never became angry, even when we would let off steam by singing the choruses and hymns at the top of our voices and deliberately off-key. Auntie Jo seemed to understand that kids needed to be a little uncontrolled at times, just to test their limits—so she just played the piano more loudly to drown us out.

Because Auntie Jo was so understanding, we came to respect her. We learned never to take advantage of her kindness, although at times we pushed it to the limits, and we came to love her so much that we would have done almost anything for her. She was our favorite adult, almost like a second mother—only we showed her more respect than we showed our mothers!

I attended Sunday school under Auntie Jo's supervision from about age four until I was a young adult. I was converted partly through her influence and as an older teenager became a lay preacher in the circuit of which our church was a part. Then, about the time I turned seventeen, I learned something astounding about Auntie Jo.

That was the year my grandmother died of stomach cancer. She and my grandfather lived in a country town about a hundred miles away, and my younger brother and I had vacationed with them every school holiday.

Shortly after my grandmother's death, my mother asked me to sit down and listen to what she had to say. She then proceeded to tell me a story that deeply impacted my life and left an indelible impression in my memory.

Mother told me that when my great-grandfather had died there had been a family blow-up concerning the terms of his will. My grandmother, his daughter, had wanted a certain family heirloom, and she was furious when she discovered it had been left to her younger sister. She swore she would never ever speak to that sister again—a promise she kept to her dying day.

My grandmother had also threatened to disown my mother and father if they ever revealed the identity of her younger sister to us children. So we grew up unaware that this great-aunt existed.

"Now what I want to tell you is this," my mother continued. "Auntie Jo is your grandmother's younger sister. She is really your great-aunt."

I was completely unseated. Auntie Jo, the person we kids all loved and admired, was my flesh and blood! I could hardly believe it.

Then a dark cloud settled over me as I realized that my grandmother, a devout Christian woman whom I had also loved and respected, had carried such a deep resentment and unforgiving spirit all those years. How could anyone be so bitter? My feelings about my grandmother turned to anger as I rushed off to find my beloved Auntie Jo and tell her I now knew the secret. Realizing that she had kept that secret from me all those years, just to protect my relationship with my grandmother, made me love and respect her more than ever.

Since that day, I have learned that my grandmother is not the only person to carry a grudge like this. Through the years I have heard scores of similar stories. I have even been guilty myself of holding feelings of resentment toward someone for a long period of time. We are all vulnerable in this respect.

RESENTMENT DESTROYS HAPPINESS

In retrospect, I now see that my grandmother was a very unhappy person, and that her unhappiness was probably directly related to her resentment and grudge-keeping. Deep within the archives of her heart she had stored the memory of a hurt she would not let go of, and that memory had eaten away at her soul.

What puzzled me about the whole affair was that my aunt was not the culprit! She had not done the hurtful act; it had been my great-grandfather's doing. But, as so often happens, resentment had distorted the facts, and the blame had landed on the head of an innocent victim. Resentment had poisoned my grandmother's thinking, and thereafter she had seen all sorts of evil intentions in the motives of other people. The result? She became and remained to her dying day an unhappy person.

Resentment *always* does this—it harms the one who holds the resentment more than the one for whom it is intended. It is the "cancer" of the emotions, diminishing our capacity for life and devouring the self just like the cancer that devoured my grandmother's stomach. She never discovered that happiness results from letting go of resentment and learning to forgive.

Is there someone in your past who has hurt you? Take a moment to reflect about it. Perhaps you recall an alcoholic father who frightened you as a child, or a mother who dominated you, or a former spouse or friend who betrayed you. We all have memories of people who have hurt us.

Now listen carefully to the implications of the principle: *You will never be a happy person unless you learn to let go of resentment and forgive every one of these people!* Forgiveness is one of the essential keys to happiness.

THE NEED FOR FORGIVENESS

In recent years, much about forgiveness has been written in Christian literature and the secular press. There is even an International Forgiveness Week (the second week of February every year) instigated by a former assistant Secretary-General of the United Nations. Can you imagine what could be accomplished on an international basis if it was really believed and practiced? But forgiveness is clearly *not* the dominant force in international relations. And that's not surprising; since we practice it so rarely on a personal level, how can we possibly expect nations to forgive each other?

During the last International Forgiveness Week I designed a "Forgiveness Certificate" on my computer. This certificate was not intended to be given to anyone else; it was strictly for the benefit of the forgiver. The idea was to fill in the name of the person you want to forgive, sign and date the certificate, and then file it away in a safe place where no one can read it. (Giving the certificate to the person being forgiven would probably offend that person and end up doing more harm than good.)

I showed the certificate to my colleagues during a faculty meeting to illustrate the value of having a concrete symbol for the act of forgiveness. Then, a little later in the meeting, I discovered that someone had sneaked the certificate away from me, filled in my name as the "forgivee," and sent the certificate around our conference room so that everyone could sign it. Finally it was returned to me, with much laughter all around.

I decided to keep that certificate in my Bible! As Dean of the Graduate School of Psychology, I need all the forgiveness I can get! We all do—because we are all imperfect people who hurt others from time to time.

But more important, we need to forgive—for several reasons. And one of the most important is that being able to forgive is crucial to our mental health.

A MENTAL HEALTH PUZZLE

Forgiveness is not a concept secular psychologists talk much about. A student of mine recently surveyed a large number of psychology textbooks to see if they dealt with the topic of forgiveness. She found absolutely no reference to it in more than a dozen basic psychology textbooks!

Doesn't this strike you as strange? Does it mean that forgiveness plays no part in mental health? Or is it that secular psychology just hasn't discovered the way to forgiveness? From my experience, I tend to believe the latter—and this is backed up by what the same student found when she went on to survey more than five hundred clinical psychologists from all across the country about their understanding of forgiveness.

Interestingly enough, a full 90 percent of the psychologists surveyed said they believe that forgiveness is an important issue in psychotherapy, and 95 percent said they often talked about it with their patients. Yet very few could agree on what forgiveness involves, and few had any clear idea of how to help people to forgive.

What a strange paradox! Psychologists on the whole agree that forgiveness is important, but no textbooks even discuss the topic! And psychologists have to help people forgive but don't really know what forgiveness is or how it can be achieved.

OUR UNFORGIVING NATURE

I believe there is a reason for this paradox. Human nature—and I mean the "old" fallen nature the apostle Paul talks about—does not really *want* to forgive the hurts it receives. It would much rather take revenge, even if that means holding on to hurtful resentment for half a century, waiting for an opportunity to pay back the hurt. I know this from personal experience and I've seen it at work in a score of patients over the years.

Fortunately, the gospel cuts right across this natural tendency. The law of the Old Covenant may have fueled the tendency to revenge, but the New Covenant refuses to allow us this destructive luxury!

Under the old law, the principle for dealing with hurt was simply an "eye for an eye and a tooth for a tooth" (Matt. 5:38). Revenge was the rule of law. You could pay back "measure for measure" every hurt you experienced.

Under the New Covenant the rules have all been changed. We are commanded never to "pay back evil for evil" (Rom. 12:17, NEB). In effect, God has said, "In your old state you were allowed to take revenge and give expression to your resentment. In your new state, I will do the punishing around here. I will repay those who unjustly hurt you. All I want you to do is forgive them." Read Romans 12:10–21 and Matthew 5:38–48 very carefully, preferably in a modern translation, if you want a clear picture of how God requires us to deal with our resentments. His prescription for our happiness could not be clearer. It is our lower nature that prevents us from understanding this prescription fully and obeying it.

WHY FORGIVE?

Several years ago, in 1984, *Time* magazine presented as its cover story the attempted assassination of Pope John Paul. The article asked the question: "Why forgive?" And it set forth a powerful rationale for why people must forgive other people if we are going to live happy and peaceful lives. Whoever put that edition of *Time* together understands the principles of the gospel a lot better than many Christians I have encountered. I would like to quote one very important extract:

> The psychological case for forgiveness is overwhelmingly persuasive. Not to forgive is to be imprisoned by the past, by old grievances that do not permit life to proceed with new business. Not to forgive is to yield oneself to another's control. If one does not forgive, then one is controlled by the other's initiatives and is locked into a sequence of act and response, of outrage and revenge, tit for tat, escalating always. The present is endlessly overwhelmed and devoured by the past. Forgiveness frees the forgiver!*

This is the clearest statement I have yet read on the value of forgiveness.

Why do we forgive? Because God told us to—and also because forgiveness is the only way to let go of old hurts that will continue to make us unhappy. Forgiveness is God's requirement for peace and justice. And it is also His loving gift to us—because we need all the protection that forgiveness can give us.

These are all powerful reasons why we must forgive. But perhaps the most important reason of all is found in the parable of the unjust (or unforgiving) servant found in Matthew 18:21–35. Peter had asked Jesus how many times he should forgive someone who had sinned against him. Peter was willing to settle for seven times, but Jesus set no limit when He replied, "Until seventy times seven." Then He told the parable of a servant who was forgiven by the king for all his debts, even though they were enormous, but who would not forgive a fellow servant's small indebtedness.

The point of the parable is very straight: The servant had been forgiven by the king, and he in turn should have shown mercy on his fellow servant. So likewise God expects us to forgive "every one his brother their trespasses" (v. 35). This establishes a clear relationship between the forgiveness we receive from God and the forgiveness we are expected to give to others.

Every time we pray the Lord's Prayer, we affirm this relationship. "Forgive us our debts, as *we* forgive our debtors" (Matt. 6:12). We forgive because God forgives us. And conversely, if we refuse to forgive, we block our own forgiveness and must live with all the consequences—including our unhappiness.

---

* *Time*, 9 January 1984: 33.

In my opinion, this is why so many formulas which promise the achievement of happiness either fail or are superficial: They fail to abide by God's conditions for personal and eternal reconciliation. The gospel is, as always, tuned right into the heart of the dilemma of human existence.

FORGIVING AND FORGETTING

A saying my mother used to throw at us kids whenever we fought was "Come on now—forgive and forget." This always puzzled me. "Why," I asked myself, "must we forget? If I forget, I might get hurt again!" Since then, however, I have come to understand a little better the interesting connection between forgiving and forgetting.

The ability to forget is a wonderful gift that we often devalue. To be able to remember everything is not always healthy. (This should be a comfort to those of us who are beginning to become forgetful as we get older!)

Henri Bergson, the great French philosopher, was quite right when he said, "It is the function of the brain to enable us not to remember, but to forget." Now, he was not encouraging absent-mindedness. He was simply pointing to the fact that life is full of potential for hurt and misunderstanding and we cannot store up all of this pain and expect to remain happy. Somehow these hurtful memories should be done away with as quickly as possible.

If we could quickly and completely forget the hurts that are done against us, we could be at peace and happiness would come more easily. But let me put that "if" in capitals—IF we could forget! Unfortunately, as most of us have discovered, it's not that easy. Resentment has the power to prevent us from forgetting, so we need another way to help us dispose of our hurts and keep the door to happiness open.

This "new" way is forgiveness—the way of the cross. And here we see the connection between forgiving and forgetting: If we can forget the hurts we have suffered, we really don't need to forgive. *It is because we cannot forget that we have to forgive.* There is no other road to happiness!

Unfortunately, even if we do forgive, we may never forget the hurts we have suffered. But if we have forgiven—truly forgiven—it really won't matter, because forgiveness will have removed the sting from the tail of our memory scorpion. The remembered hurt will no longer have power to perpetuate the resentment that can be so damaging to our minds and spirits.

HOW DO WE FORGIVE?

But *how* do we forgive? That is really the crucial question, isn't it? It's one thing to talk about the value of forgiveness and quite another thing to put forgiveness to work in our lives.

Perhaps the most helpful guideline for how to practice forgiveness was one I heard many years ago, when I was in my mid-twenties. A dear friend, a missionary in Africa who was then approaching the end of his missionary service, was preaching on the topic of forgiveness to a large group of black African believers. His topic was timely. Many, if not all, of his listeners had suffered significant deprivation because of racial prejudice. Most had been deprived of equal justice and opportunity all their lives and had every reason to be angry. Their hurts were plentiful and significant, and they were quite vocal in their resentment.

How could these people ever forgive the wrongs that had been done to them? How could they ever have peace in their hearts when all their natural instincts prompted them to take revenge for deep hurts?

In answer, my missionary friend pointed the imagination of his listeners to a Jesus on the cross who had also been despised and rejected. He showed them in vivid imagery the nail-pierced hands and bleeding side of the Son of God who had come to bear all the burden of their pain. He warned them that more nails and more bleeding sides were to be their portion before they could ever see justice and racial hatred abolished.

How were they to live until this time of justice arrived? His answer was simple and forthright—in forgiveness! They were to heap forgiveness on the heads of all those who perpetrated injustices.

He then went on to define forgiveness in a way that has stuck with me ever since and has proven to be extremely helpful to myself and the many patients I have worked with down the years. He said, "Forgiveness is surrendering my right to hurt back."

What a clear definition! And what freedom this brings to make forgiveness possible!

My friend's definition suggests two answers to the "how" of the forgiving process.

First, surrendering your right to hurt back asserts that *you do have a right to feel hurt* and even to repay the hurt against you. Unfortunately, many of us try to forgive others by denying or minimizing the hurts they have caused us. "Oh, they didn't mean what they said" or "They didn't know what they were doing" or "It really doesn't bother me that much" are responses we use to play down the intentions of others or our reactions so as to forgive more easily. Unfortunately, this is a tactic recommended by many Christian teachers.

The trouble is, forgiveness by denying or minimizing the hurt doesn't work. Instead, it "short-circuits" forgiveness because it entrenches our resentment even deeper.

One reason is that the kind of self-talk we give ourselves in such situations is often simply untrue. For instance, often people who hurt us know very well what they are doing; they mean every twist of the knife! But even if the hurt is unintentional, it is still real, and denying it won't make it go away!

The first step to forgiving others, therefore, is to recognize and acknowledge the hurt done to you. It *is* real! It *does* hurt! Quite likely, the other person *did* mean what he or she said!

You can only forgive if you know to the fullest extent the hurt done against you, so take a while to review what has happened. Claim your right to feel hurt and your right to pay back the hurt. Here are some important "don'ts" for this first step:

- *Don't* try to channel your anger elsewhere. It deserves to be where it belongs.
- *Don't* ignore the hurt feelings you are experiencing. They won't go away.
- *Don't* try to forgive at this point by initiating some act of reconciliation. You may only cause more hurt.
- *Don't* try to forget the hurt by absorbing the pain and disappointment. Forgiveness comes before forgetting.
- *Don't* minimize your hurt. Experience it to the fullest so that you *know* what it is you must forgive.

Now, comes the second step. When you fully understand your hurt and accept that you have a right to feel this way, then *surrender this right back to God,* just as Christ did on the cross. Give it up! Lay down the axe you have lifted to take revenge.

Why? Because God has asked you to—and because it is necessary for your own happiness. Relinquish your need to even the score. Abandon your lower nature's urgent need for repaying the injury and for wounding your aggressor. This is the act of forgiveness.

Forgiving is clearly something you *decide* to do. Resentment is spontaneous as well as poisonous and destructive; it requires no conscious decision. But forgiveness is an act of your will, a determination of your mind that you make with God's help.

THE FRUITS OF FORGIVENESS

What happens when you make the decision to forgive rather than live in resentment?

You probably won't feel better right away—the right feelings come only after you've behaved in the right way, not before. You probably won't even feel less angry at first. Anger subsides only as the threat of an emergency diminishes. But you will have done what God wants you to, and this is all that matters.

And then, gradually, you can start to dismiss the feeling of being wronged and clean out the injury files you have used to collect the hurts done against you. You can even begin to absorb the pain and disappointment of lost friendships or broken relationships. And slowly—you can begin to forget!

Forgiveness isn't easy—but it works! So do not wait for others to apologize before you forgive—you may wait forever. Always be the first to offer the hand (often the secret hand) of forgiveness, and you will be the first to see happiness bloom again.

To be able to forgive completely, with no residual need for revenge, has to be the noblest, most beautiful form of love. It comes closest to the heart God demonstrated when He forgave all our sin. Forgiveness works miracles, brings untold peace and guarantees a deep happiness.

HELPFUL THOUGHTS

Here is a weeklong program for achieving this happiness through forgiving. Each day, concentrate on a different aspect of your life where forgiveness may be necessary:

Sunday   Work at forgiving yourself. Anger at self far surpasses all other forms of anger as the destroyer of happiness.

Monday	Think of each member of your present family and forgive each one individually for any hurts he or she has caused you.
Tuesday	Think of the members of your extended and past family—including those who are deceased or distant—and forgive each one.
Wednesday	Forgive your friends and neighbors. They can be a major source of resentment.
Thursday	Forgive your work colleagues, your fellow club or class members, and other closely related groups.
Friday	Forgive the company where you work, the government, and other corporate bodies for all the injustices caused you, both intentionally and unintentionally.
Saturday	Thank God for the power He gives you, in Christ, to forgive others. Confess any anger you have toward Him and pray again for His forgiveness of you.

Happiness Is Living in the Here and Now

I VIVIDLY REMEMBER MY first day in elementary school. I was five and a half, and I sat near the front behind a girl who giggled her way through every class period.

I was miserable! School was too confining; it robbed me of my freedom. I remember saying to myself, "I am unhappy here. Surely this isn't what life is about. One day when I get to go to the big school I'll be happy."

By "big" school, of course, I meant high school. I knew that all the big kids went there, and they seemed very happy. So I struggled through the next seven years waiting for the next stage of my life to open to me, certain that the next stage would be really satisfying.

Eventually I arrived at high school, and again I can remember that I wasn't pleased with how it turned out. I said to myself, "I am unhappy here. This isn't what life is about. But never mind, when I go to the university I'll be happy."

At the university, I said to myself, "When you earn your first real paycheck—then you'll be happy." Carrying my first paycheck home (I don't even remember how much it was), I said to myself, "When you get married, then you'll be happy." Then it was "When you have children . . ." and "When your kids are grown . . ." and "When you get that new car. . . ."

And what I am finally beginning to learn after all these years is this: You cannot wait until the next stage of your life to be happy—it must start now.

When does life *really* begin? When do we finally start living or arrive at happiness? In school? At work? When we are married? When the children are grown? When we get that promotion or develop that relationship? When we make our fortune? When we retire? When we get to heaven? It is very easy and seductive to get so caught up in the belief that happiness is just around the corner that we never find the happiness that is available to us now!

THE "TOMORROW" SYNDROME

I have come to believe that many of us are caught in a trap of *living unhappily in the present because we believe the future will be happier.* I call this the "Tomorrow" Syndrome—we are sure everything will be happy "tomorrow." But the reality we must come to understand is that unless we can find happiness in our present circumstances, we will certainly not find it in the future.

Do you remember *Annie,* the musical that was so popular a few years ago? It is a moving story, based on the comic strip "Little Orphan Annie," about a girl who is able to bring happiness to everyone, herself included, despite the fact that as a baby she had been abandoned to a cruel world.

The hit song from that musical is called "Tomorrow." The heroine sings it with great gusto to cheer up the other characters when they are down. It's an interesting song with a clear message of hope, promising that no matter how bad today is, tomorrow will be better.

When I first heard that song, I was a little down. Things in my life weren't going quite as I had planned, and I clearly remember reacting positively to the idea that my unpleasant life circumstances would soon pass, that "tomorrow" would be better. I resonated with Annie as she continued to sing about how days that are gray and lonely can be turned into sunshine by just sticking out your chin, grinning, and saying, "tomorrow. . . ."

I left the show feeling great! But soon afterwards the lyrics of that song began to bother me. I recalled Paul's words to the Philippians:

> Not that I was ever in need, for I have learned how to get along happily whether I have much or little. I know how to live on almost nothing or with everything. I have learned the secret of contentment in every situation, whether it be a full stomach or hunger, plenty or want (Phil. 4:10–12, LB).

As I reflected on Annie's encouragement that tomorrow would bring out the sun, I realized that Paul had a better idea: we can achieve contentment in *every* situation. Annie's song doesn't really help much, because we really have no promise that tomorrow will be better! All too often, the next day just brings more unhappiness.

Unless we learn how to make the most of our "today," sunny or gray, crowded or lonely, we will never be able to find happiness in our future. If we look for it tomorrow, happiness will always be *one day away!*

Now, this does not mean we are not to have hope! Paul himself spoke of having hope as an "anchor" (Heb. 6:19), and the theme of our hope in Christ runs throughout the Bible. Certainly, as Christians, we live in hope of Christ's future coming.

But hope does not mean putting off all happiness for some nebulous tomorrow. If we live in the hope of Christ's coming, we also rejoice in the present joy that He has already come! And that is enough to assure us happiness in the here and now—we don't have to wait for tomorrow to be happy!

It's very easy to let yourself get stuck with a lifetime of cloudiness or loneliness. I know many whose life circumstances are not likely to change—people whose bodies are broken or who have lost loved ones and opportunities. Unless these people learn how to be content "in every situation," especially their present circumstances, they will never be happy. And that goes for those of us who are more fortunate, too. Delayed happiness is no happiness at all.

THE "LATER" SYNDROME

Now, of course there are many circumstances that *can* be changed. I am not suggesting that you helplessly leave your conflicts unresolved or that you take no steps to remove your pain. Unpleasant work situations, unreasonable bosses, and unresponsive friendships that are destroying you *should be changed*. Failing to take steps to make things better is patently self-destructive. If you do this, then you only have yourself to blame for your unhappiness.

But this suggests another side of the "living in the here and now" question. Some people, rather than expecting to find their happiness in the future, try to find their happiness in the present by putting off *action and responsibility* "until later." This is *not* what I mean by finding happiness in the here and now! This is procrastination—what I call the "Later" Syndrome. And it can make us as unhappy as living in the future does.

The tendency to procrastinate is as old as creation and is very strong in most of us. It is even socially accepted, and the few who conscientiously do everything right away are often labelled as "compulsive." But not all compulsiveness is bad, as we will see.

Whether the task is confronting a friend for some hurtful remark, returning an unpleasant telephone call, doing our taxes, or fixing a leaking faucet, we would rather do it "tomorrow" than now. But unfortunately, these "tomorrows" also may never come, so the unpleasant chores pile up like snow on a highway and eventually bring us to a halt. Our "mañanas" are our undoing!

Why do we procrastinate? I suppose one major reason is that *delaying an unpleasant task seems to relieve us of some of the anxiety* associated with that task. For the moment we don't have to face any unpleasantness. But the problem of course is that putting off the task only prolongs the anxiety. We've been fooling ourselves!

For example, I hate returning telephone calls. I used to collect all the yellow message slips my secretary would give me at the end of each therapy session and pile them high on my desk. I discovered that with 50 percent of them, if I ignored the message for long enough, the need to call back went away! Somehow the person who called resolved his or her need to talk to me. It was an interesting discovery!

But while delaying the unpleasant chore of returning calls relieved some of my anxiety, it prolonged the remaining tension until eventually I had to face making the balance of the calls anyway. Nights were spent in sleeplessness anticipating what had to be done, so I finally decided it was far better to return all my calls as soon as possible.

Then I made a more important discovery. If I made all the calls and cleared away all my yellow slips before going home in the evening, I felt happier and less tense, and I could anticipate the next day with greater joy. My discomfort was considerably reduced if I performed the unpleasant task as soon as possible. Putting off the inevitable definitely did not make me happier.

I know a woman who is chronically unhappy. Throughout her childhood and adolescence, whenever she experienced difficulties or felt anger, her mother would say, "Go and lie down, dear, and you'll feel better." This became a lifelong habit. She was taught by her loving but overprotective mother to avoid direct contact with problems or confrontation with people. The result is that she spends a lot of time in bed and is unable to engage life realistically.

Another reason we procrastinate is that *we have bad discipline habits.* Lack of personal discipline will create enough chaos in your life to sabotage your happiness.

Discipline is a necessary ingredient in all successful accomplishments. The student who lacks control over distractions or the pastor who lets secondary obligations crowd out regular study time will suffer much disruption and discomfort from this lack of control.

Now, I am aware that in emphasizing that lack of discipline underlies much procrastination I may be pushing some guilt buttons, and at a later point in this book I will show how to deal with excessive or destructive guilt. But feeling *some* guilt over this matter is probably necessary if you are going to enjoy the happiness that can come when you learn not to procrastinate.

If you have a procrastination problem, try not to wallow in self-pity or self-punishment. Instead, accept your failure objectively and *design a change.* All happiness depends on your ability to take constructive steps to correct whatever defects or inadequacies you perceive in your character. The integration of your successes and your failures—especially your failures—into your total experience is essential to deep and abiding happiness.

THE "IF ONLY" SYNDROME

Come now, admit it—you often say, "If only I *had* . . ." or "If only I *hadn't*. . . ." We all live with regrets, regrets about decisions made or not made, regrets about actions committed or not committed. And this is a third kind of problem we may have with finding happiness in the here and now. Instead of living for the happier future or putting off positive action until later, we may ruin our happiness by dwelling on what did or did not happen in the past.

It is impossible to go through life with straight As in every aspect of your life. Somewhere, somehow, when you least expect it, mistakes will creep up on you and temptation will overcome your best intentions.

Underlying the "If Only" Syndrome, our tendency to wallow in regrets, is the erroneous belief that we should never make mistakes. We fear that people will think less of us if we are not perfect or that making mistakes is a sign of weakness. Such a belief is a major obstacle to happiness because it creates unnecessary anxiety in situations where we fear failure or feel neurotic guilt over our lack of perfection.

Mistakes can be blessings in disguise, providing not only necessary experiences, but desirable ones as well. How else will we be able to correct our deficiencies? How else will we grow to maturity?

Every one of us has the *right to be imperfect*, to make mistakes and not be blamed for being human. If you are to be happy, you must claim this as a fundamental right to your existence. And that means refusing to dwell on past mistakes.

THE VALUE OF THE JOURNEY

Living in the "here and now" means enjoying the journey of life and not being so preoccupied with its destination.

When we first married, my wife and I moved far away from our hometown; we had to travel about four hundred miles every time we wanted to visit our parents. There were few freeways in South Africa at that time, so we made the journey over narrow, winding country roads in an old English-made Austin.

The first time we made the journey, it took us twelve hours at an average of about thirty-three miles an hour. (Today you can do it on a freeway in five and a half hours!)

I never enjoyed that long trip! Even as we left home to start our trip, I would begin to focus on the destination. How are we progressing? How far is it still? How much time to go? What time will we get there? I fretted all the way!

It helped that there were many little towns along the way. Each one represented a milestone on the journey, and I could check them off in my mind with relief as we passed through them.

No matter which route I took, I always arrived at our destination exhausted, because I had not yet discovered the value of *enjoying the journey*. In my haste to get where I was going, I paid little attention to the gorgeous countryside or the interesting towns. All I saw were milestones and the ultimate destination. Sad! But some of us take longer than others to mature.

I often apply this story to the lives of my students—now that I know its lesson. I warn them that our graduate program is long and arduous, and that if they focus only on finally getting their Ph.D., they will be miserable and miss the wonderful experiences on the way. If they are going to survive six years of hard work, they must learn to enjoy the process itself. Each moment of every day must be made to count—or the goal just won't be worth it.

This is life. What matters is the journey, not just the destination! Whatever you do *now* is what must make you happy, not what you expect to do when you reach a certain stage of life or accomplish a particular goal. And to continue the analogy of a journey, getting to the end of your life is not the point. Enjoying the travel in-between *is*.

I am happy to report I am now able to apply this lesson in my own life. A year ago, while visiting our daughter and son-in-law in Germany, my wife and I had the opportunity to visit the Bavarian Alps. Driving the *autobahn* at high speed, I caught myself in my old habit of wishing we were at the end of our journey, and paying little attention to what was happening in-between. So I suggested to the others, "Let's not hurry on to the next city, but stop here in one of the little towns nearby and enjoy some local color." With some persuasion they agreed, and we pulled off into a little village that was not on our itinerary. We found a small "Gast Haus" for the night, ate a delicious supper, and strolled around a quaint German village far off the usual tourist route. The experience turned out to be one of the highlights of our visit.

The lesson? Learn to savor the journey. Take time to enjoy what you are doing *right now!* Whether you are washing clothes or writing a report, completing your homework or painting a masterpiece, changing a diaper or feasting at a gourmet restaurant, *enjoy every moment!* This is the only way to find happiness on life's long journey. If you wait until you have achieved your goal before you seek to be happy, you will wait a long time—perhaps forever!

Scripture has a very clear word for us here. We are told to "redeem . . . the time" (Eph. 5:16 and Col. 4:5). Literally these verses mean to "make the most of every opportunity." This is the attitude of the wise—you make every moment count, and you don't put off your happiness to some future time.

The most important moment in life is *now*. Life is short enough, and if there is anything to be done, do it now, "for the night cometh when no [one] can work" (John 9:4).

When you are young, life seems to know no limits. But soon days run into weeks and weeks into years. Quickly we come to the point that there is more distance behind us in the journey than ahead. If we miss one day, it is gone forever. So grasp this minute! Hold it tight! Redeem it, for it is precious.

A happy life must be lived in the joyful present. Certainly, plan for a happy future, prepare for your security, and make provision for a rainy day or your retirement. And remember your past with pleasure, enjoying happy memories as you put past mistakes behind you. But unless you develop the habit of enjoying the present, you will not find happiness, now or then. Living each day to the fullest—accepting the challenges and blessings each day brings with grace and faith and believing God is with you every moment—will guarantee a life of joy.

HELPFUL THOUGHTS

Donald Marquis once wrote, "Procrastination is the art of keeping up with yesterday." Living in the "here and now" also means that we should keep up with today! Here are some ways to overcome procrastination:

- *Always tackle unpleasant tasks first.* Once you have completed these, completion of the easy tasks will follow naturally, and you will always have a sense of being up to date.
- *Never believe that if you avoid problems and unpleasant situations today, they will go away tomorrow.* They only get worse when you avoid them.
- *Avoid the erroneous "positive-thinking" idea that "everything will work out fine."* Most situations will only work out all right if you make them work out right.
- *A common cause of procrastination is the fear of making mistakes.* We would rather not act than act wrongly. This fear immobilizes many of us. The only way to overcome this fear is to take risks and believe that mistakes are necessary for growth.
- *Stop striving for perfection.* You cannot do everything perfectly so you might as well learn how to do things *reasonably* well and be content. Accept that all human beings, by their nature, are imperfect and fallible.

For those having problems in how to find happiness in present circumstances, here are some suggestions:

- *Avoid fantasizing about how things could be better or reliving past failures.* Whenever you catch yourself saying "If only . . ." or "I should have . . ." or "I wish I hadn't . . ." remind yourself that all you have control over is the present. Focus on actions you can take rather than regrets and self-recriminations.
- *Don't envy those you think are better off or happier than you.* You don't know the whole story of their life, nor do you

know what problems are about to befall them. In prayerful dependence on God's Spirit, say to yourself, "I choose to be happy with who I am and what I've got, here and now." Repeat it to yourself until you begin to believe it.

- *Set aside a regular time each day to reflect on the enormous power of God in the universe,* demonstrated throughout history, and available to you *now!* Ask God to help you make the most of every opportunity and make every moment count.

Happiness Is Appreciating
the Little Things

A RECENT ASSOCIATED PRESS RELEASE was headlined, "Americans Said Healthy but Feel Lousy."* The report went on to say that Americans have never been healthier, but that they feel worse and worse—a phenomenon that has become known in medical circles as "the paradox of health." Despite the fact that the nation's collective health has improved dramatically over the past thirty years, people report a general dissatisfaction with their physical states.

What is behind this? I think that even though we are healthier and live longer—in 1900 life expectancy was forty-seven; now it is seventy-five years—our increased longevity has only given people more time to experience unhappiness! How else can you explain the paradox that industry reports twice as many episodes of disabling illness per capita in the 1980s as it did in the 1920s *before* the introduction of antibiotics? People don't want to work. They find little real happiness in their life's calling. They search for real joy, yet rarely find it in any aspect of their lives.

I believe there is a fundamental reason for this. It is the same reason why, even as our society has given us bigger and better gadgets—faster cars, more elaborate toys, more colorful TVs, and racier entertainment—we have become more unhappy. To our detriment, we have forgotten how to appreciate the little things of life!

I have a minister friend who experienced a heart attack two years ago. He is a charming and charismatic person. He is also high-pressured and dynamic, and he can outpreach anyone I know. But early heart disease knocked him flat. He discovered that his pursuit of the "big" issues in life was killing him. So after open-

---

* "Americans Said Healthy But Feel Lousy," *Star News*, 18 February 1988.

heart surgery which replaced three coronary arteries, he learned to slow down.

During his post-surgery recovery, my friend would go into his backyard and sit quietly, enjoying the fragrance of the flowers and trees and basking in the warm sun. During one of these rest times he caught sight of a family of blue jays who had set up their nest in a tree just near him. Never before had he noticed them; in fact, he had never known that birds lived in his yard at all! Before long, he found himself eagerly looking forward to getting home from work so he could quietly watch the blue jays go about their business. It thrilled him to observe them coming and going, building a nest, fighting over a morsel of food, and enjoying the life God had given to them.

My friend was gradually coming to realize that life involves more than charging headlong to self-destruction. The words from the Sermon on the Mount resounded in his mind: "Take no thought for your life, what ye shall eat, or what ye shall drink. . . . Behold the fowls of the air: for they sow not, neither do they reap, nor gather into barns; yet your heavenly Father feedeth them" (Matt. 6:25–26). And a great peace came over him. It was finally clear to him that there is more to life than preaching to big crowds in huge auditoriums, important as that may be. Accomplishing some great task or traveling to distant lands to minister to others is no more important than watching a bird in his garden.

Sitting in his backyard after a heart attack, my friend found the foundation of happiness. If he could come to value the comings and goings of birds, he would be able to accomplish all of God's calling without premature self-destruction. He needed to experience the "little things" to help him accomplish the "big things."

WHAT HAVE WE LOST?

While reviewing a major textbook on mental disorders in preparation for a class I was to teach, I came across these words: "Children typically seem to feel happy, whereas grownups do not." And the truth of this statement penetrated my mind as it never had before. We start out happy in life, most of us, but we end up unhappy. Why? Something goes wrong on the way!

The author of the textbook goes on to explain that children are more spontaneous in their social behavior than adults and that their natural mood is more elevated and joyful. Putting it simply, the textbook said, children know how to enjoy themselves, and growing up teaches us how to stop being playful.

But I think there is more to it than this. Children are happier also because they know how to enjoy the "little things" of life. We tend to lose this ability as we get older, and so we become less happy.

I recall my own early childhood. I grew up during World War II, and during the war years there were no toy factories—every resource was being applied to the war effort. A child could not buy a kite, gun, bicycle, or chewing gum, no matter how much money he had. We had to create our own toys, and as I reflect back on how we did this I think we derived greater pleasure from our crude, self-fabricated playthings than my children ever did from their factory-made equivalents. We made cars out of tomato-box wood. We shaped toy soldiers out of sunbaked clay. We invented gadgets from bottle tops, cotton-reels, and string. We were forced to be creative and to use our imagination more than children are today. Toy manufacturers could probably make a fortune by recapturing this need in children and devising toys that would force them to be creative. They should sell kits of odds and ends and challenge our children to be original in their creations.

The point here is that "little things"—the simple pleasures of life, and those we devise ourselves—can give us much more pleasure than big and expensive things. When realistic toys became available after the war, they were discarded by us kids within hours of receiving them. They bored us, just as they bore my young grandsons now. Is it any wonder then that these days we grow healthier, but more miserable? If we do not notice birds, smell roses, or watch sunsets, we can never expect to be truly and deeply happy.

ENJOYING THE "LITTLE THINGS"

Life is full of "little" things to enjoy. Friendly glances from strangers on the sidewalk, a tender moment with a child, a long-awaited letter, or the fresh fragrance of the earth after a rain—all these are "little things" not because they are unimportant, but because they cost nothing—they are absolutely free!

One evening last spring I was walking past a house in our neighborhood when I caught the whiff of a flowering shrub. Instantly a flood of early childhood memories overwhelmed me. I had not smelled that scent since I was six or seven years old, but the memory of it was deeply locked into my mind, and smelling it again instantly brought forth all sorts of happy thoughts related to my childhood.

I stopped in my stroll and lingered for a while near that bush just to be able to enjoy its fragrance. When I had set out on my walk I had been angry. It had been a hard day. Everyone had been against me (or so I thought). But as I enjoyed the fragrance and the memories it evoked—stooping to break off a twig of blossoms and hold it closer to my nostrils—my tension left me and my composure was restored. Smell may be a "little thing," but it can be enjoyed to the point of making a person feel sane again.

We are constantly gifted with a stream of "little things" which can help restore our mental and emotional balance and provide us with a rich resource for happiness—if we learn to appreciate them. In addition to enjoying nature, which contains the greatest store of happiness-producing opportunities, we can enjoy the creativity of others through music, poetry, art, and books. And let us not forget the important gifts of Scripture and prayer—they are both ours for the receiving.

THE BLESSING OF SOLITUDE

I could focus and expand on many obvious "little things" that can give pleasure, but I will leave my readers to explore these themselves. Instead, I would like to address two less obvious ways of enjoying the little things of life, because they are often overlooked and undervalued in our hectic and hassled existence. And the first of these is *the blessing of solitude.*

Most of us do not naturally seek after quiet and solitude. We have a deep-seated desire for excitement, a constant need for stimulation. When we go to church, we desire to be entertained more than we want to worship. When we sit down in the evening to relax, we want to be diverted by a TV thriller or comedy. Inactivity scares us. Being alone frightens us. We tend to look at solitude as a form of punishment. We can no longer tolerate being alone with ourselves.

But when you study the great saints of Christian history, one characteristic stands out: They all were able to achieve enough "aloneness" to be able to hear God's voice; they discovered that they were closest to God in stillness—not in the clamoring, activity-filled pressures of their lives. In this they were following the example of their Lord, who throughout His ministry was in the habit of withdrawing to a quiet place to pray (see Matt. 14:23; Luke 5:16, 9:18, 22:39–46) and commanded His disciples to do likewise (Matt. 6:6).

From a Christian "spiritual formation" perspective, the transforming of our love, desires, and behaviors is primarily achieved through discovering the power of God and His ability to renew our whole beings. There can be no substitute for time spent in deepening prayer life and in communing with God. But such communion must be done *in solitude*—by yourself.

God is the friend of silence, the companion of those who can still their clamoring imaginations and quieten their discomforting memories. Solitude, moments spent with God as your only companion, is a precious gift. And if you can develop a capacity for it, solitude can be a powerful and positive modifier of your personality.

Now, obviously, to be alone all the time can be devastatingly painful and not necessarily beneficial. But being unable to tolerate any solitude results in never coming to know yourself and never learning to commune with God at a deep level.

Have you noticed that we have less reason to be bored than our ancestors, but we are more afraid of boredom? We constantly bombard ourselves with stimuli to take away our boredom—TV, radio, newspapers, and the neighbor's gossip. Unfortunately we have come to believe, even in our most devout evangelical circles, that times of quiet and inactivity are not part of natural existence, and that excitement and challenge must constantly be our goal. We pay for this with increased stress disease and a diminished capacity for, and experience of, happiness.

Furthermore, as I have shown in my book, *Adrenalin & Stress,* when we crave excitement, we can actually become addicted to it, to the point that we need ever-increasing doses of it to satisfy the craving. Thrills become stale, and new thrills must take their place. This can take the form of "adrenalin addiction," in which we come to depend on an elevated level of adrenalin in our bloodstreams. Whenever this high level of adrenalin subsides, we tend to become melancholy—we get the "post-adrenalin blues"! And so we look for more stimulation; we "pump" ourselves up to get that "adrenalin high" that comes with overstimulation.

The problem with this, from a health point of view, is that over a period of time elevated levels of adrenalin lead to heart disease, high blood pressure, and other stress-related problems. But in addition to undermining our health, the addiction to excitement tends to dull our palates for the ordinary experiences of life. Simple things—the love of a pet, the beauty of a sunset, a stroll down a quiet street, or even the fragrance of new-mown grass—no longer please us. And this is true of our spiritual lives also. We reach the point where the peace of God's constant presence must be fortified with a "sign" or other overt evidence of His power, or else we are disappointed! His still, small voice cannot be heard above our clamor for thrills and excitement.

As parents, we must take much of the responsibility for passing this "addiction" on to our children. A mother I was counseling recently complained because her daughter loved to sit quietly in her room reading a book. "Shouldn't she be out playing with her friends?" she asked. "Shouldn't she be getting rid of pent-up energy and doing what everyone else is doing?"

"Perhaps," I responded. "But it would be preferable if you encouraged her in being alone sometimes. She has a precious gift. Don't take it away from her."

A generation incapable of appreciating quiet and solitude will be a generation of people who are spiritually deaf, with no ears for God, and spiritually mute, with no voice to sing His praises. Certainly there'll be no capacity to achieve happiness. Listen again to a hymn you probably sing often, for it contains an important key to being happy:

> Drop Thy still dews of quietness,
>   Till all our striving cease;
> Take from our souls the strain and stress,
>   And let our ordered lives confess
> The beauty of Thy peace.*

THE BLESSING OF THANKFULNESS

The *second*, less obvious, way of coming to appreciate little things is through understanding the value of thankfulness.

Scripture, again, is not silent here. Exhortations to thankfulness are so frequent in Scripture that I hardly know where to begin. First of all, our thankfulness is to be offered to God. We "enter into his gates with thanksgiving, and into his courts with praise" (Psalm 100:4).

But there is another spirit of thankfulness that can help us to

* John Greenleaf Whittier, "Dear Lord and Father of Mankind."

achieve an appreciation for the little things of life. It is an essential ingredient in developing a happy spirit. If you never pause to reflect thankfully on your blessings, no matter how few or small, you will never know how blessed you are. Thankfulness needs to be a conscious, *deliberate* act of your mind. It is *frequently* an act of worship, the sacrifice of your heart. I will have more to say about this kind of thankfulness in a later chapter.

HELPFUL THOUGHTS

Teach yourself how to focus on and enjoy the "little things" of your life by deliberately attending to Nature around you.

- Take time to go alone into your garden or local park and study some activity of nature. Watch the ants collect food, the birds build their nests, or the squirrels forage for nuts.
- Listen to the sounds around you—the wind in the trees, or the distant honking of taxis or buses. Try to sensitize your ears to the little sounds and block out the loud ones.
- Close your eyes and feel the wind in your face. Then pick up a leaf and run your fingers over the surface. Feel the texture of the leaf—how different it feels above and below. Focus on touching other things and notice how often you fail to attend to your sense of touch.
- Smell the air and attend to a variety of scents that come to you—even the unpleasant smells. What do they remind you of?
- Focus your thoughts on what is going on around you now. Try to get your mind off troublesome problems for this brief period and pray, thanking God for His handiwork that is so evident in every part of His creation.

Happiness Is Living
with Reality

MY PARENTS DIVORCED when I was twelve. If you have never experienced divorce from a child's point of view, you don't have the slightest idea how much pain, humiliation, and despair a marital breakup can involve. For me the experience was worse than death; it spelled the end of my world.

It's not that the divorce was unexpected; for years our home had been a virtual battlefield. But despite all the unpleasantness, I would rather have had my family intact than broken up. I could live with strife, I felt; I could not live with uncertainty and the scattered quality of the life which followed.

The divorce had a devastating effect on my emotions. Because I was a boy, I would not allow myself to cry. If, in a moment of weakness, a tear would begin to fall, I would quickly wipe it away and hide my shame. But inside I felt excruciating pain as I watched our home being torn apart. It wasn't a wonderful home, but it was still home, and it had given me security. I had to say goodbye to the friends I had grown up with. I feared that my mother would be unable to support us. How would we ever survive?

In the months that followed, I turned to the only way I knew to cope with my aching heart: I began to fantasize. I had a vivid imagination, and I discovered I could create, in my mind, any world I wanted. The nightmare of the divorce and the separation from my father could easily be overcome in fantasy. So I retreated to my inner world where I spent hours in fairy-tale bliss, making everything work out as I wanted it to. In my imagination I could conjure up a happy home, reconcile my parents, and build a bright future—and I did. I imagined all sorts of happy endings to our life-story. After a while, my fantasies became mixed with prayers. Every night I would put myself to sleep with a mixed fantasy and prayer that when I woke up in the morning all would be well.

But of course when morning came, the painful reality was still there, and I became even more unhappy because I had gotten my hopes up. It would have been better if someone had taken the time to help me accept the inevitability of my parents' break-up and to adjust to reality. If this had happened, I believe, I would have returned more quickly to a happy state of mind. For true happiness requires the ability to live in harmony with reality.

FACING REALITY

Nothing meaningful is gained by ignoring reality. You cannot wish your world into changing, nor can you imagine away your problems. Most of us know this fact, but not many of us have faced it squarely! We prefer to deny or ignore our problems rather than confront them realistically, and as a result those problems never go away.

We all do this to one extent or another. Have you ever avoided getting on the scale because you were afraid you had gained a pound or two—or left the mail unopened when you thought it might contain bad news? In fact, avoiding reality is a dominant whole theme in our culture—as evidenced by the countless advertisements which promise that this product or that product will make us beautiful or keep us young. People in our society are terrified of growing old, and we cling tenaciously to the illusion of youthfulness, even though aging—and death—is inevitable. Rare is the person with the maturity and mental health to leave one stage of life and graciously accept the reality of the next.

The variations on the theme of avoiding reality are endless. Ideas such as "positive thinking" and the success myths of "health and wealth" so prevalent in our modern Christian ideology are popular because they provide hope that we can transcend our reality-bound existences. Movies, novels, TV, and even some preachers present us with distorted ideas about what life is really about. We either live as if life was one long fantasy, or we harbor a deep, though unconscious, suspicion that everyone else is getting a better deal—either way, we distort reality to avoid facing up to it.

But we *must* learn to accept reality if we want to live a happy life. Of course, we could argue until doomsday about what reality is, but then we'd be missing the point. Thomas Merton, in the opening remarks of his book, *Thoughts in Solitude,* * says, "There

---

* (Farrar, Strauss & Cudahy, 1958), p. 1.

is no greater disaster in the spiritual life than to be immersed in unreality." This is true for *all* of life. To ignore the reality of a lump in the breast or an aching tooth can be physically disastrous. Hiding from the reality of deep anger toward a loved one can lead to psychological problems. And denying the reality of sin in our lives is devastating on a spiritual level.

Life can only be lived to the fullest when we engage reality to the fullest. Only then can we take charge of what is happening to us and set about to change it. To deny reality or to escape into fantasy or wishful thinking will never solve a problem or equip you to overcome a hardship.

When our lives are immersed in unreality, we stagnate. When our lives are fed from unreality, we starve. Without having something which gives or sustains *real* life, we inevitably experience unhappiness. Unreality, fantasy, and wishful thinking are nothing more than mirages in the desert, dry and dusty places that give the illusion of beauty and growth, but that vanish when we are again faced with the hardship of our lives.

Now, when I speak of "unreality," I am not talking about fantasy or imagination as an occasional diversion or a creative exercise. Our imaginations are gifts from God, and they can be rich resources for enjoyment and for problem solving—and for understanding realities that are deeper than those we can perceive with our five senses. It is when imagination and fantasy are used to avoid facing up to problems in life that they become barriers to real and lasting happiness.

THE GIFT OF REALITY

The greatest gift you can give yourself is the gift of reality—the determination to live within the real world, courageously facing each problem with the will to overcome it and not run away. The more directly you confront the givens of life, the happier you will ultimately be. Passiveness and helplessness always lead to despair. It is my prayer for you that you will come to love reality.

We are all consummate dreamers. We would rather have fairy-tale happy endings than grow from the pain of unhappy ones. We love turning our disappointments into a fantasy of wants and wishes, but it is reality that brings out the best in creativity from us, that causes us to draw upon God's resources in a new and growth-producing way. Truth about our world is better than untruth. Truth can set us free, whereas avoiding truth will only make us more miserable.

I tried to deal with the catastrophe of my parents' divorce by retreating into fantasy. Because no one helped me to look at reality and make the right sort of adjustments to it, I became depressed. A cloud hung over my emotions throughout my high-school years and well into my twenties. Only when I began to build a happy marriage for myself did this cloud begin to disperse. Only as I began to discover the value of engaging reality solidly did I begin to build the skills necessary for coping with the hardships of life. Life then began to take on a new meaning. Every moment of my life became precious. I stopped wasting time wishing things were different, and I set about changing them so they became different. Life became thrilling, and my appreciation for what God was doing took on a new depth.

God can help us cope with life as it really is, not with life as we wish it to be. He wants our feet on the ground, so we can walk in His way.

WAYS WE AVOID REALITY

Human ingenuity is boundless, and it benefits us greatly in terms of medicine and technology. But it is also boundless when it comes to avoiding unpleasant reality—we human beings can find all sorts of ways to avoid reality.

One of the most common means of these is *denial*—unconsciously convincing ourselves that a situation simply doesn't exist.

A patient I was once seeing in therapy came in one day and announced that he had just come from his physician. He had not been well lately and so had had a number of tests carried out.

"My doctor thinks I may have leukemia," he announced. "But I don't believe he knows what he is talking about."

I was stunned not only by the sad news but also by my patient's seeming lack of concern for the seriousness of his condition.

"What are you going to do about this?" I asked.

"Nothing." Plain and simple—nothing! He had decided not to go back to the doctor who, he said, had a "negative thinking style"!

At first I wasn't sure whether the sickness really was serious enough for further investigation. Maybe his doctor *had* been wrong, and I should just let him be! As we talked, however, it became clear that my patient was in denial; he claimed the sickness didn't exist because he did not want to face its reality. If he avoided further tests, his unconscious mind reasoned, he wouldn't have to face the sickness. But I pointed out to him that the leukemia would come about whether or not he faced its reality, and gradually he became more willing to do what he could to fight the disease. Whatever the reality of his illness, he was better off facing it than running away. At least he could seek out the best treatment.

This kind of denial is a very common defense against reality. Sometimes it is unconscious, so that the person isn't even aware of the denial. More and more, however, I am finding that it *is* conscious, but that people just refuse to look at reality because it produces too much pain. This kind of denial is a form of wishful thinking. Mothers deny the reality of the pills they discover in their teenagers' bedrooms. Wives deny the reality of telltale signs of unfaithfulness. Christians deny how sin affects their spiritual lives.

Denial is very comfortable, and it's very easy to learn. Just say to yourself, "It doesn't exist," or "I'll just ignore the evidence," and you can have a healthy dose of it right at your fingertips.

Excessive denial can give rise to a very serious group of emotional disorders called "hysterical conversion" disorders. In these cases, the inability to face painful reality causes the conversion of anxiety symptoms into psychological forms of paralysis, amnesia, blindness, loss of voice, and even seizures. Denial is also a contributing factor in "multiple personality disorders," where two or more distinct personalities coexist within the same person. The sudden change from one personality to another is often brought on by the stress of some painful reality; often the "other" personality knows nothing about the problems of the first. Reality is "compartmentalized" to such a degree that psychological comfort is maintained by escaping to another personality. Imagine this! Every time your real world becomes too painful for you, you switch that world off, change to another personality, and start a new life! Not very healthy, but it temporarily avoids pain. Unfortunately, it also prevents one from ever coming to terms with real problems.

Another way in which we avoid reality is a mechanism called *intellectualization*. This manner of avoidance is the favorite of educated people and those who feel threatened by emotion. With intellectualization, emotionally disturbing aspects of the real world are kept at bay by treating them in a detached, objective way. The person who intellectualizes escapes from a world of emotions into a world of ideas and words—and he or she is usually unaware of what is happening.

Let me illustrate. I once knew a minister whose wife could no longer tolerate his putdowns and criticisms. For most of their married life, she had been made to feel inadequate. She wasn't smart enough, he said, to understand his ideas, nor was she quick enough to keep up with his facile mind. Whatever she said, he criticized. No doubt he did this because of his own deep-seated insecurity and low self-esteem. He needed to look good in comparison to somebody, so he chose his wife. When she could take it no longer, she walked out on him and demanded a separation.

As I began to talk to the husband about his feelings shortly afterwards, it was clear that his wife's leaving had hurt him deeply. She was the only one who had understood and tolerated him. Yet he would not admit that he had abused her love. He launched into a long explanation (an intellectualization) of why she had done what she had done, and none of it had anything to do with himself: "She's just been under too much stress in her work." "She's not had a good vacation for years." "She's missing our oldest daughter, who has gone off to college." "She doesn't understand that all marriages have some problems." He reeled off the excuses one after another, unable to face the reality that he had treated his wife shabbily over many years just to appease his demanding ego.

The more this man tried to be detached and objective about his wife's leaving him, the deeper he dug the hole for his pained psyche. Finally he struck bottom, burst out crying, and sobbed himself back to reality. We were then able to begin the therapeutic task of exploring the real reasons why his wife had left him. The process back to health and happiness had begun.

COMING TO GRIPS WITH REALITY

The more we embrace reality and seek to work in collaboration with it, the happier we will finally become. But before you reach the happier mountains on the other side, you may well be required to go through a valley of unhappiness. "No pain, no gain" is not just good advice from an athletics coach; it is also true for spiritual and psychological growth. Confronting reality is not for cowards!

Looking honestly at yourself—your wiles and waywardness—is never pain-free. Seeking to understand the real reason for a failure in your marriage, for missing a school grade, or for not making a promotion will never be easy. But there is no other gateway to abiding happiness. From honest reflection on your life's reality will come a more determined will to change and a fuller understanding of what needs changing.

How can we engage reality more effectively? *First,* we can ask God to help us set aside all the *defenses* we have built against it. I have illustrated denial and intellectualization, but there are other defenses as well; in fact psychologists have identified about sixteen different ones.

"Projection," for instance, means blaming others for your troubles. A common projection is to blame your parents for all your problems. Unfortunately, some forms of psychotherapy encourage this. And it may be true in a few cases that a parent is partly to blame for a child's troubles. But even in these cases, the child must eventually take responsibility for his own behavior and stop blaming others—including his parents—in order to grow. My parents were not the greatest. But if I lose my temper, it is not their fault, but *my* responsibility. *I* have to correct it. Blaming my father because his bad temper rubbed off on me is neither healthy nor helpful.

"Displacement" is another defense against reality. Here we take out our anger on an innocent person or object. Another term for this is "scapegoating," after the Old Testament practice of choosing a live goat, symbolically placing all the sins of the people on it, then chasing the goat out into the wilderness to carry away all the sins of the people (Lev. 16:20–22). When *we* scapegoat, we force someone else (a spouse, kids, the cat, or a close friend) to take the brunt of the guilt for an unhappy situation, even if they are not the cause of it.

So, first, pray that God will release you from these defenses against the reality of your life.

Second, in the words of the well-known "Serenity Prayer," ask God for courage to change what can be changed and the serenity to accept what cannot. *Both* parts of the prayer are essential. There is much that we *can* change if we have the courage to step out and take the necessary steps. If you don't know what or how to change, then seek competent counseling. Don't be afraid to talk over your problems with a trained Christian therapist. There are very few problems we can reason through by keeping them to ourselves. An objective outsider can help us stay in touch with reality.

There is also much we *cannot* change. If this is true, we must learn to *accept it*. Failure to accept that which cannot be changed only leads to unhappiness.

Allow me to give a personal illustration. I have always been self-conscious about my height—or at least my lack of it. My grandmother was short. My father was short. But I am the only offspring who is short.

I first became aware of my lack of height at about age twelve. Up until then I was the tallest boy in the class; then I stopped growing, and everyone else whizzed past me.

I keenly felt that being short was a handicap. (I've since discovered that many tall people consider it to be a handicap to be tall!) My height limited the number of girls I could date and the positions I could play in sports. So I began to pray, as a teenager, that God would help me to grow again! It was a prayer God never answered.

Later in my adult life, I came to terms with my height and realized that unless I came to a place of complete self-acceptance, I would never be a happy person. A young graduate of the seminary at which I now teach helped me come to terms with my height twenty-six years ago. He told me that he had had a similar problem with the shape of his nose—and up to that point I had not even noticed his nose! After our conversation I went home and changed my prayer from "God, help me to grow" to "God, help me to accept that which I cannot change."

This time God did answer my prayer—once I faced up to reality.

HELPFUL THOUGHTS

Here are some ideas to think about:

- *Living with reality* is waking each day to the miracle of your life and its limitless possibilities.
- *Living with reality* is developing a deep sensitivity to the grandeur of human life and accepting that both joy and sadness are necessary.
- *Living with reality* puts us in touch with our hopes, dreams, and longings and helps us understand and reach them.
- *Living with reality* keeps us mentally alert to all that goes on in our lives and warns us of where change is needed.

- *Living with reality* stretches our minds and shapes our characters to greater maturity.
- *Living with reality* is the behavior of courageous, honorable people seeking to be fully alive and constantly enlarging their vision.
- *Living with reality* means always seeking to harmonize our desires with God's purposes for us.
- *Living with reality* means we use all the resources that God provides to build a joyful and happy life.

PRINCIPLE EIGHT

Happiness Is Keeping Your Expectations in Check

WHY DO MOST PEOPLE expect more than they can get? Why do they set themselves up to be disappointed simply because they allow their expectations to far exceed what can reasonably be delivered?

I am as guilty as anyone. Each day I used to make a list of things that I needed to do—letters to write, people to call, and so on. Most of the time it was a long list, and by the end of the day I had barely succeeded in getting through a quarter of it.

Instead of feeling good about all the tasks I had accomplished, I found myself feeling unhappy because I had not completed everything I had placed on my list. Instead of just seeing the list as a guide for what had to be done, I took the list as an absolute mandate. I ignored the reasonableness of its length or the kinds of tasks it contained. My expectations were out of control. I expected myself to be the superman of chore completion, merely because I had compiled a list a mile long. My expectation was that no matter how long the list of tasks, I had to do them all *that day*. And I had no patience with myself if I did not comply!

To remedy this tendency I experimented with two approaches: I could *shorten* the list to a point where I could complete it every day and even do a few extra chores not on the list to make me feel better. Or I could *lengthen* the list to a point where I could not reasonably accept it as a challenge for any one day; I would have to see it as a long-term project. If I took the second approach, the list would simply be a guide for work to be done, not an expectation for that particular day.

Not too surprisingly, both techniques worked. I stopped demanding more of myself than could reasonably be completed in one day of work, and my level of happiness increased.

97

UNREASONABLE EXPECTATIONS
CAUSE UNHAPPINESS

Making long lists of things to do each day may not be a major problem for many readers. Some may suffer from the reverse problem, namely, not having any list at all; you have great difficulty motivating yourself to get *anything* done! (I also know this feeling at times.)

But my concern here is less with "outward" expectations such as "To Do" lists, and much more with the many "inward," unreasonable expectations that cause chronic unhappiness. Unfortunately these internal expectations are much more subtle and powerful in their influence. They tend to be "abstract" and hard to identify, and they have to do with what we or others "ought" to be doing in order to prove our goodness or our love. Such expectations are rarely expressed clearly even to ourselves; they tend to dance around in our minds as assumptions—"I always need to be perfect" or "If he loved me he would send flowers."

We are all saddled with these impossible *internal* expectations. Our parents teach them to us. Our culture fosters and adds to them. Television and the movies exaggerate them. Our educational system reinforces them. We cannot escape coming into adulthood without a host of unrealistic or illogical internal expectations batting around in our minds, waiting to make us unhappy every time they are not met.

UNREASONABLE EXPECTATIONS IN MARRIAGE—
AND OTHER RELATIONSHIPS

Nowhere is the unhappy influence of unreasonable expectations more devastating than in marriage. Because of the closeness of the marital relationship, expectations operate at an intense level. Our marriage partners, more so than anyone else, are subjected to a constant flow of demands and expectations.

One of the unfortunate consequences of our culture's overemphasis on romantic love as the basis for marriage is that we tend to idealize our lovers during the dating period. We attribute romantic qualities to them and do not see them for what they really are. (And, of course, they are on their "best behavior" during this time.) We transfer onto them all our unmet past needs with the expectations that these needs will now be met.

If we were deprived of a certain form of love in our childhood, for instance, we now expect our partner to replace that love. If we were humiliated as a child, we need our partner to praise us constantly. Positive experiences also build expectations—if our needs have been met in a certain way, we expect our partner to continue the practice to which we are accustomed. For instance, if our mother showed love to us by bringing us breakfast in bed, we may expect our spouse to show love the same way.

We bring, therefore, a host of expectations, reasonable and unreasonable, to our marriages. We have an "ideal" image of what our spouse should be (because this ideal best meets *our* needs), and then we set about trying to squeeze him or her into the mold of this ideal. They must become what *we* want him or her to be, rather than becoming who he or she really is. When the gap between the "ideal" and "real" is too great in our partner, we begin to "fall out of love." Resentment builds if our spouse does not change to match our expectations, and conflict may ensue. If our partner *does* meet our expectations, feelings of love will probably continue, but this love may be unstable because it depends on the partner's continuing to fit our idealized expectations.

There is always a gap between our expectations of what a spouse should be and the reality of what that spouse is. This is a given! Unless we change our expectations and stop trying to change the person we married, we will never achieve real happiness in our marriage.

Let me give you a very personal illustration of this. When my wife and I dated, I idealized her to a great extent. As a child I had been somewhat deprived of love. While my mother was a good provider of material things, she had experienced too much pain in her marriage to my father to be able to give much direct love to my brother and me. So I brought to my marital relationship an excessive need for my bride to demonstrate her love all the time. I transferred to her my need for constant reassurance and an unlimited emotional presence. I expected her to focus her energies on me and on no one else. I resented her friendships with others and wanted her to be solely my friend.

These were unreasonable expectations, and they rapidly brought unhappiness. It was unfair of me to expect Kathleen to lie down in the mold of my making and conform to every corner and detail.

It took many years of personal struggle before I began to modify my expectations for Kathleen, to allow her to be her own self—not just the meeter of my neurotic needs. As she grew to be more fully herself my expectations changed, and our love matured. Similarly, my wife brought to our marriage many expectations which were of her making. She, too, had to go through a similar process of maturing.

Much so-called "incompatibility" in marriage is actually a discrepancy in the expectations each partner brings to the marriage relationship. Such incompatibility is inevitable, since each person in the marriage comes from a totally different background and with wholly different needs. In a way, marriage is always a relationship of unlikely partners, even when they seem very much alike. Differences in genes, upbringing, and experiences will assure a certain degree of incompatibility in every marriage.

What marriage partners are called upon to do, by adjustment and personal growth, is to work out the differences in expectations together and to free each other from expectations that are neurotic and unreasonable. I believe it is a fallacy to say that incompatibility destroys a marriage; as G.K. Chesterton wrote in his essay, "*What's Wrong With the World,*" "If people can be divorced for incompatibility, I cannot conceive why all of us are not divorced. I have known many happy marriages, but never a compatible one. The whole aim of marriage is to fight through and survive, the instant when incompatibility becomes unquestionable."

Of course, marriage is not the only sphere of life impaired by unreasonable expectations. All relationships are affected. This is why love is so important to humans. Love, real love, helps to water down the devastating effects of expecting others to always do our bidding. It helps us forgive those who fail to meet our expectations. And when we fail to measure up to our own expectations, it can help us forgive ourselves. Not only must we give others the freedom to become more fully themselves; we also need to give ourselves that freedom. We can only be what God has created us to become; to expect something different is to court unhappiness.

EXPECTATIONS COME FROM THINKING

We *are* what we think. We *do* what we think. We even *look like* what we think! Furthermore, we are no more spiritual or righteous than we are in our thinking: "As [a man or woman] thinketh in his heart, so is he" (Prov. 23:7).

These statements are both frightening and comforting. They are frightening because they remind us that our thoughts are the reflection of our character. We are no more than what we think, so if our thoughts are unholy and perverse, then our character is likewise unholy. The correlation is a perfect one!

They are comforting statements, on the other hand, because if I am the sum total of how and what I think, then by shaping my thoughts I can begin to shape my character so that it can become whatever I want it to be. And while my mind has been "renew[ed]" when I became a Christian (Rom. 12:2), I cannot just leave it to chance that my mind will become whatever it needs to become. I can shape and form it by discipline, giving it the direction it requires to become a generator of thoughts that will both please God and create a healthier mind (Phil. 4:7–10). I have to "[bring] into captivity every thought to the obedience of Christ" (2 Cor. 10:5).

Our expectations, good or bad, are the product of our thinking. They are created, shaped, and evaluated by our minds. That means that we can manage our expectations; we are not at their mercy.

When I expect everyone I know always to respect me and show me that respect by believing everything I say, I have created this expectation *in my mind*. The only way to change this (or any other) expectation is to change the way I have programed my thinking.

If expectations come from our thinking, then unreasonable expectations come from *bad thinking*. By "bad" I really mean uncritical or unexamined thinking. Too often we go about our thinking without ever stopping to examine our thoughts. We would never allow a gas station attendant to put water in our gasoline tank; we know it would foul up the engine. Yet we pay little attention to what we pour into our minds and the "foul-ups" we create there. Scripture directs us very clearly to "Keep thy heart with all diligence; for out of it are the issues of life" (Prov. 4:23). In this scripture, as in many others, the word translated "heart" really means the mind, not the literal blood pump in the middle of the chest, and not just the emotions. The mind is the center of our being, and it must be guarded and cultivated.

As far as our unreasonable expectations are concerned, we need to examine our thinking often and call our expectations into our consciousness for examination in the light of our walk of faith. When they cause us unhappiness, they need to be challenged and removed both by prayer and decisions of the will.

I once counseled a client (let's call her Carol) who was unhappy about her relationship with a friend. She had a certain set of expectations about how a friend should affirm and support her—but again and again those expectations were disappointed. Whenever she made a decision about a personal matter, she would seek out her friend and share the decision with her, only to receive in return a comment of criticism or a put-down about her decision. Whenever Carol had a difficult conflict to deal with at work, she would tell this friend about the incident, and the friend would always find some fault in the way Carol had reacted. No matter what problem she shared, her expectation that the friend would be understanding and affirm her for her reaction or decision was never fulfilled.

After many years of so-called "friendship," Carol finally realized something was wrong and sought counseling. As we reviewed the relationship, both of us could see clearly that the friend's refusal to be affirming grew out of her own history of deep personal hurt. In finding fault with Carol, she was really venting a deep-seated anger that had nothing to do with Carol. This situation was not likely to change, so if Carol continued in her expectations, she was doomed to unhappiness with her friend.

I told Carol she could choose between two courses of action. She could abandon the friendship, which never seemed to hold out any promise of being mutually supportive anyway, or she could change her internal expectation that the friend would affirm her in her times of distress. "Take your pick," I encouraged her, "but you must make a choice. One thing is certain; you cannot continue to experience repeated disappointment without destroying your own happiness."

Carol cried for a while. Then she said, "I know my friend has a problem of her own and cannot deal with my issues impartially. But I would rather keep the friendship than throw it away. I suppose I must stop expecting her to always support me in whatever I do."

And Carol did begin to change her expectations of this friend, and a few months later she reported a dramatic breakthrough in their relationship. The friend, now seeing that she was not being set up to always be approving, began to confront why she always rejected Carol's decisions and reactions. She admitted to herself and Carol that she had a problem and began to deal with it. Carol had saved the relationship by changing her expectations. She grew more mature and helped a friend find more happiness.

DOWNGRADE YOUR EXPECTATIONS
OF OTHERS

I keep a sign in my office that a client once gave to me. It reads, "Blessed are they that expect nothing, for they shall be satisfied."

Now there are two ways you can interpret this sign. One way is to understand it as saying, "Don't bother to attempt anything. You won't succeed anyway, so if you don't try, you won't be disappointed."

This is *not* what it means. This is a defeatist attitude, and I certainly don't encourage it. The way the sign is intended to be understood is "Trim down what you expect from others to a reasonable level. If you do this, you will find ways that people *do* live up to your expectations and make you and themselves happy."

I call the technique I often use to teach this "bonus building."

For instance, if I am excited about meeting with an old school-day friend I haven't seen for many years, I can prepare myself by expecting him to be extremely nice to me, respectful, free of all jealousy, and uncritical. But I might be disappointed. How do I know he hasn't changed? How do I know he won't be critical of me? How do I even know whether or not he still feels friendly toward me?

Now if, instead of unreasonably building up my expectations that he will be a "super" guy, I merely accept that time has changed both of us and that we are not the same any more—if I don't expect the encounter to be extraordinarily pleasing—and our reunion turns out fantastic, *I have created a bonus*. If it doesn't, I haven't lost anything and will not be disappointed.

Put simply: It is almost always better to accept people and life events at face value without inflating them in our expectations. If we do this, we are almost certainly going to receive a bonus—and be happier. If we don't do this, we will often be disappointed.

Build as many bonuses into your life as you can, and you will be a happy person. I don't mean that you should be a pessimist and always expect the worst. If you are a negative-thinking pessimist, you probably won't recognize a bonus when it comes. I merely mean to be reasonable in your expectations and trim them down to the level of reality.

Don't be a killjoy or a cynic. Simply be realistic. Don't let your wishful thinking run away with fanciful ideas about what to expect from others; you will always be disappointed.

OUR EXPECTATIONS ARE IN CHRIST

There is only one realm of thinking in which unlimited expectations are reasonable and lead to happiness—our beliefs about how Christ can work in us and what we can expect God to do for us.

Read Ephesians 1 again, paying very close attention to verses 3–14. Here we are told of the superlative spiritual blessings that are ours through Christ: "[We are blessed] with every blessing in heaven because we belong to Christ" (v. 3, LB).

Is this possible? Is this really what Paul means? *Every* blessing that is in heaven can be ours *now*? It sure is! The very idea sends thrills up my spine—and in some small way I feel I have already experienced it.

Listen to some of the wonderful "bonuses" we are promised in this passage: "his wonderful kindness to us" (v. 6); "because of what Christ has done we have become gifts to God that he delights in" (v. 11); and "His presence within us is God's guarantee that he really will give us all that he promises" (v. 14). The New International Version translates verse 14 like this: "[the Holy Spirit] is a deposit guaranteeing our inheritance until the redemption of those who are God's possession." This means that there is more to come!

How can we hold back our expectations here? And yet we do! This is the amazing paradox. We build our expectations for this life and for what people can do to and for us to an unreasonably high level, and yet we restrict our minds when it comes to believing what God can do for us. We tend to humanize God and deify our fellow creatures. We reduce God to our human limits but expect people to be as perfect as God. What strange creatures we are!

God has promised us "every blessing in heaven"—and He keeps His promises. So allow your expectations to soar—He will live up to them, and more!

HELPFUL THOUGHTS

Here are some important do's and don'ts about expectations:

Do Not Expect:

- To receive more love than you give to others.
- To never make mistakes nor give expression to your humanness.
- To be always understood by others.
- To be able to please everybody.

- Others always to do your bidding.
- Always to be right and never make mistakes.
- To succeed without taking risks.
- To be able to live independent of others.
- To be approved by others for what you stand for.
- To experience happiness without working for it.

What You Can Expect:

- God will always be faithful.
- God will not always give you what you want, but He will answer your prayers.
- God will always be there when needed.
- God will forgive you for being human.
- God will give you strength to follow *in His steps.*

Happiness Is Being Yourself

I HAVE A THEORY. I believe that most of us, if we are absolutely honest, would prefer to be someone else—or at least be different from what we are. I've tested this theory a few times in classes and seminars, and it seems that most people won't admit to thinking this way—but I really believe they do!

So many of us are dissatisfied with the person God made us to be. We may envy other people and wish we were like them—we may even spend an inordinate amount of time daydreaming we *are* the person we admire. Or at very least, we wish we were taller or shorter, thinner or fatter, fairer or darker, quieter or more outgoing than we are.

When I was eight or nine, I desperately wanted to be someone else. Do you want to know who? I wanted to be an Arab sheik. I was totally enamored of flowing robes and impressive headpieces. I wanted to be able to jump on a horse and ride off into the desert night, singing songs and sleeping under moonlit skies. *Desert Song* was my favorite movie. I'm serious! I wanted to be a sheik—until I changed my mind and decided I would rather be a cowboy!

Now, this kind of wishing is not unhealthy for children—it exercises their imaginations and helps them sort out who they really are. But when it continues into adulthood it can be a barrier to happiness—because being happy requires that we come to terms with the unique person God made us to be.

Evidence for the idea that we have great difficulty just "being ourselves" comes from many sources. Take plastic surgery, for example. Plastic surgeons exist, for the most part, to repair self-esteem by correcting physical features people are unhappy with. True, sometimes the corrections are necessary for health reasons, but mostly they are done because the patient believes he or she will be more acceptable with a lower hairline, smaller nose, firmer chin, or more voluptuous bust.

Look also at the tremendous popularity of "self-help" or "self-growth" seminars these days. Instruction on everything from overcoming the "fear of succeeding" to "building greater self-confidence through juggling" is swallowed by gullible and disillusioned people who are desperately unhappy with who they are. (Unfortunately, for these well-intentioned souls, problems of low self-esteem or, as I prefer to call it, "self-hate," are deeply rooted within their beliefs and attitudes and require a lot more than a weekend seminar!)

Now don't get me wrong. I don't believe there is anything wrong with wanting to improve yourself by changing your appearance or learning new skills. In many cases such "self-improvement" can be quite beneficial—but only if first you learn to accept yourself as you are. So before you reach for the Retin-A jar to smooth out those wrinkles or enroll in a body-building course, take a long look at yourself in the mirror and resolve to come to terms with the you God made you to be.

We are not created to spend our lifetimes trying to be someone else or become something we are not. Instead, God intends that we discover our own individual uniqueness and then live out this uniqueness before Him with His help, doing His work. When we fully cooperate with this process, we are at our happiest.

The Living Bible translates Romans 5:2 with great beauty and clarity:

> For because of our faith, [God] has brought us into this place of highest privilege where we now stand, and we confidently and joyfully look forward to actually becoming all that God has in mind for us to be.

Isn't this beautiful? God has something in mind for us to "become." He wants us to "be" something of His design. But it is *not* an imitation of someone else; He wants us to be fully ourselves.

WHAT "BEING YOURSELF" IS NOT

"Be yourself" is a cliché that is much bandied about these days, but it is often misconstrued to the point that many of us shy away from it. We are afraid it might mean becoming preoccupied with our own needs or becoming self-centered and we don't want that.

But selfish preoccupation is *not* the same as "being yourself"—and it has never opened a door to happiness. In fact, the very drive to be someone else, as I have been describing it, *is* self-preoccupation. The desire to be stronger, prettier, taller, or lighter (for anything but health reasons), bespeaks an unhealthy focus on oneself.

It is very common to feel this way when you are growing up. But one of the signs of maturity is that you become *less preoccupied* with yourself and your wish to be anything but yourself. Self-acceptance is a higher level of spiritual and psychological maturity than self-rejection or an obsession to change who you are.

"Being yourself" is *not*, therefore, a greater level of self-concern. Quite the opposite. Happy people are able to enjoy life because they don't fear being themselves. They have dismissed their fantasies of greatness or extraordinary success and can live in the moment, fully acting out God's plan for their lives in their own unique way. They don't meditate on their sins, follies, and shortcomings. They accept forgiveness readily and seek to change their lower nature with the help God provides.

"Being yourself" is also *not* a greater level of self-interest. It is not dominating your world and insisting that others "do it my way." It certainly is not focusing on meeting all your own needs at the expense of the needs of others nor riding rough-shod over the sensitivities of others.

"Being yourself" is *definitely* not license to be obnoxious. A spouse of a ministerial student at our seminary recently shared with my wife her feelings about what was happening to her husband. Due to the pressure he was experiencing in school (and on the advice of a counselor), he had begun to act out his frustrations at home. He would explode in anger whenever his wife did something he didn't like. When she pointed out that he was very tense and super-sensitive, he would defend himself by saying, "I've just got to *be myself!* When I'm angry I need to just express my anger. That's who I am—take it or leave it!"

This isn't emotional health (as some therapists might suppose)—it's quite the opposite! Being oneself is not a matter of giving expression to every impulse of anger—or any other impulse either, including the sexual impulse. You are not being "true to yourself" when you do this. You are threatening your own happiness and the happiness of all those around you.

If we all felt that we had the right to explode every time we feel frustrated or hurt, we would create a chaotic world around us.

We must, of course, be honest about our feelings. When we feel angry, we should be able to recognize and accept our anger, for only then can we take the necessary steps to correct whatever is causing the anger. But blaming others, and more especially, punishing them when you are angry, is a different matter. This is not being "true" to your real self, but surrendering yourself to your lower nature—an act of ultimate self-depreciation.

No, being yourself does not mean self-concern, self-interest, nor self-indulgence, but accepting and being true to who you are, seeking to live out your life in the knowledge that God has designed a unique place for you in His kingdom and taking your rightful place in His "body" (Rom. 12:5). While you may have a different "gift" (v. 6) compared to that of others, your gift is uniquely yours and must be exercised with freedom.

DELIGHT IN GOD'S DESIGN

You are who God has designed you to be. Not to accept this is to run the risk of missing God's purpose for your life and ending up unhappy.

True, God hasn't finished implementing His design, but the rough shape is there, waiting for the hand of the Master Sculptor to continue His work. God will work with the "givens" to shape you into a beautiful object of His creation. Like any master sculptor, He knows precisely what treasure lies hidden within the rough shape of you. He will bring out the very best, so delight in His design and cooperate with His creative process, even if His knocking away of rough corners is painful.

Many of us are so neurotically afraid just to "be ourselves" that we hamper much of what God can do in and through us. We keep asking ourselves, "What will people think?" or "Will they still like me if I am just myself?" As I mentioned in an earlier chapter, we engage excessively in "impression monitoring"; we constantly scan the reactions of others to see what sort of impression we are making. Because we are afraid to be ourselves, we "take the temperature" of how others react to us and try to adjust to what they want us to be.

This tendency to monitor the impression we are making on others is very prevalent in Christian circles. We are very concerned about our "image" (perhaps overly so) and consequently inhibit our freedom to become uniquely who we are. We rob ourselves of our individuality and try to shape ourselves into clones of someone who is highly admired. But if we believe that heaven is going to be populated by masses of identical clones of our favorite pastor or preacher, we are going to be very disappointed!

Not only do most of us, to some extent, engage in "impression monitoring"; we also use "impression management" as a way of fitting into what we think others want us to be. We say what we think people want to hear and do what we think they want us to do. We spend a lot of time worrying whether we have offended a friend or irritated a boss. Most of this is unnecessary, and it keeps us from being our "real selves." How sad this is!

How can we grow if we cannot be ourselves? How will we ever be happy if we are constantly trying to become what others want us to be?

Low self-monitoring individuals and those who are not overly controlled by the impression they are making on others are healthier and happier and have less concern about failing. They are more willing to take reasonable risks, can express their feelings honestly, show more love for others, and grow faster spiritually. This is because they are more "genuine," both to themselves and others. They are not hypocritical nor are they judgmental. They give others the freedom to be themselves, just as freely as they claim it for themselves.

DARE TO BE DIFFERENT

To break the habit of trying to be something you're not, you may need to dare being different. Take some risks and champion your right to be you, remembering to give others the same privilege. This is the way of honesty and of love.

No one I know who has not claimed the privilege of being himself or herself has accomplished anything significant for God's kingdom. For God's people often have to stand by themselves against great opposition, and this requires a strong sense of personal identity. Christian history is full of examples of those who have dared to be different. The apostle Paul stood his ground before Herod Agrippa so effectively that Agrippa admitted, "almost thou persuadest me to be a Christian" (Acts 26:28). Martin Luther stood against centuries of tradition to start the reformation of the church. John Wesley, John Calvin, and many other great Christian leaders had to do the same. They dared to be themselves in the sense that they accepted that God had unique plans for their lives, and they had the courage to act on those plans.

By the grace of God, we must not run away from our selfhood. Rather we must accept our basic selves and then proceed to let God fulfill the creation of His image in us.

I was converted at age eighteen through the influence and love of a group of Christian young people. At the time, as part of my engineering training, I worked with other trainees in a large engineering department. And one of these trainees, a few years older than I, gave me a tough time because I had "dared to be different" and announce my Christian commitment.

I got double messages from this fellow trainee. On the one hand he wanted to be my friend. On the other he mocked me, often humiliating me to the point that I secretly shed tears.

Somehow God gave me the courage to continue taking my stand. I resisted being drawn into activities that were unsavory (such as spending time bar-hopping instead of studying). It helped greatly that I had just met my future wife, also a new Christian, and she helped me to stand firm.

For five years during my engineering training I endured the ridicule of this fellow trainee. I could not avoid him, nor did my assertive confrontations reduce his need to make fun of my Christian convictions. Then my wife and I married, and I took up a position elsewhere in the country.

Many years went by, and I lost touch with my fellow trainees. Then one day I received a telephone call. My ardent humiliator had taken an engineering position in a city just fifty miles away and wanted to meet and restore our friendship. With much trepidation I agreed to have dinner with him, and it turned out to be a remarkable reconciliation.

In the intervening years my friend had married. After the tragic death of his first child, he had begun to examine his life and his beliefs. And, he said, remembering my determination to be different in the face of much opposition had finally convinced him that there may be something in this "God-business." Now he is an elder in his church, active in personal evangelism and in discipling others. Together we thanked God for His faithfulness and rejoiced in our common faith.

Many times I am tempted, as I suppose you are, to just conform and "go with the crowd." At a more subtle level, I often have difficulty being myself and simply accepting that I am what God has created me to be. While He faithfully continues His work of sanctification, I cooperate best when I surrender *all* of me, without avoiding who I really am or fantasizing being different. I am as unique as any snowflake or any star in the sky. And it is this uniqueness that He blesses most—it is what makes me *me*. As William Shakespeare wrote in *Hamlet*,

> To thine own self be true, and it must follow, as the night the day, thou canst not then be false to any man.

BECOMING

Let me once again refer you to Romans 5:2 as it is rendered in *The Living Bible*: ". . . and we confidently and joyfully look forward to actually becoming all that God has in mind for us to be."

That word *becoming* is a beautiful word, pregnant with associations and images. It implies *direction* in our growth, showing that there is purpose and great potential in the future. I begin my "becoming" by claiming the freedom to be the individual I am and accepting and affirming my uniqueness. But I also place myself at the disposal of my Creator and Savior so that I can fulfill His divine plan for my life.

As a little child, I kept silkworms for a hobby; most kids in my town did. We traded squares of blotting paper with worm eggs laid on them every springtime and prepared ventilated shoe boxes with mulberry leaves to receive the little worms as they hatched. Every day we fed them fresh leaves until they were large and ready to spin their cocoons. In the garden I noticed other worms who were also weaving their cocoons. These other worms seemed to be ugly and useless. They ate the leaves so that the plants became ugly and even died. As a child I wondered why God even put them there!

But then the miracle happened. The worms, hidden in their cocoons for many long weeks, suddenly emerged, revealing the wonder of metamorphosis. And then came the surprise. Our silkworms became moths, and the ugly garden caterpillars became beautiful butterflies!

Granted the silk moths were not as colorful as the butterflies, but on the way they had produced the most beautiful patterns you can imagine as they wove their tiny thread of silk around any shape cardboard form you left in the box. Hearts, squares, and circles became covered in pretty silk. The butterflies, on the other hand, wove their silky beauty right into their colorful wings. It almost seemed that the uglier the caterpillar, the prettier the butterfly!

The point I am making here is that silkworms and caterpillars both are on the way to "becoming" something very beautiful, and this is an analogy we can apply to our own lives. You may not like who you are very much, but always remember that you, too, are in the "becoming" stage. One day you will emerge from the cocoon of this life, with all its uncomfortableness and inconveniences, and take your place as the beautiful creation God intends you to be.

The more you cooperate with this process, the happier you will be while you are "becoming." Don't run away from who you are—you may be destroying something very beautiful. *Be yourself fully*—it is all God has given you. Thankfully, it is more than enough!

HELPFUL THOUGHTS

The Good Self-Image

When you get what you want as you struggle for self
    And the world makes you King for a day.
Just go to a mirror and look at yourself
    And see what *That* man has to say.
For it isn't your father or mother or wife
    Who judgment upon you must pass.
The person whose verdict counts most in your life
    Is the one staring back from the glass.

He's the person to please, never mind all the rest,
    For he's with you clear up to the end.
And you've passed your most dangerous, difficult test
    If the man in the glass is your friend.
You may fool the whole world down the pathway of life.
    And get pats on your back as you pass.
But your final reward will be heartache and tears
    If you've cheated the man in the glass.

                         Anonymous

Happiness Is Being Able to Enjoy Pleasure

MARK TWAIN wrote in his *Letters from the Earth* that "Americans work harder at having a good time than at any other single endeavor." I agree. The pursuit of happiness through pleasure is probably the most common obsession of all.

We start our children very young in this pursuit. Their first exposure to Disneyland, Walt Disney World, Magic Mountain, or their equivalents in your neighborhood, start them on a life quest in which leisure and pleasure tops the list of the most important things to achieve. Later they will spend a fortune each year rooting for their favorite baseball team, cheering the latest entertainment star, finding the right jogging shoes, catching a tan, or thrilling to the smell of burnt rubber at an auto race. For most of our culture, pleasure is the game; pursuit of it is the aim.

I don't mean to imply that this pleasure is all bad—heaven forbid! Life is hard enough as it is; we need all the diversion we can reasonably get, just to lighten our load a little and maintain our sanity. In fact, as a psychotherapist I will often prescribe a night of fun or weekend of leisure to restore some luster to a dull marriage or depressed spirit.

No, the problem is not so much the desire for pleasure as in the frantic search for happiness through pleasure—especially our selfish pursuit of pleasure for its own sake. I hope I have made it fairly clear in this book that such preoccupation can make us unhappy.

But there is another happiness problem involved with the pursuit of pleasure—losing the ability to enjoy it. This is the problem I want to discuss in this chapter.

THE DULLING OF PLEASURE

In our pleasure-seeking society, it is not unusual to become anesthetized to pleasure—to overstimulate our senses to the point that they become numb and dull through overindulgence. We are tranquilized by too much novelty and excitement, and the trivial activities that constitute the primary focus of our pleasure-seeking are powerless to maintain a high level of happiness.

At the end of every day, crowds stream out of amusement parks, movie theaters, football stadiums, or bars—or they turn off the TV set, which brings this all to the armchair anyway—and the happiness they experienced (if indeed they were able to experience it) quickly fades like the bright sky at sunset. Their "pleasure centers" have been dulled from too much stimulation, and boredom quickly overcomes them.

Psychologists believe that there is actually a "pleasure center" in the brain, a point in the septal region which can be stimulated to experience pleasure. Electrodes can be implanted in this area and electrically stimulated to deliver enjoyment.

An animal, for example, can have electrodes hooked up to its brain and be taught to press a bar to receive stimulation in this part of its brain. And the animals learn quickly to press that bar! Rats have been known to press such a bar of their own accord as many as five thousand times an hour.

The drive for pleasure is so strong that hungry rats would rather stimulate their pleasure centers than eat. In one experiment, a rat pressed the bar more than two thousand times an hour for twenty-four consecutive hours. Finally it collapsed of hunger and thirst.

Obviously, human beings aren't rats, but this evidence does confirm that pleasure-seeking is a powerful drive. In fact, there is reason to suspect that pleasure centers are even more powerful in controlling human behavior than they are in controlling animal behavior.

More important, it has been shown that the pleasure center in the brain can be overstimulated to the point that it becomes numb and unresponsive. The system becomes dull and unable to react with fresh energy to sensations of pleasure. And humans are more prone than animals to this dulling effect.

I see this dulling tendency in my grandson. At five years of age, he has tremendous capacity for pleasure, but he quickly becomes satiated with enjoyment. If you take him to an exciting activity, he is at first overjoyed and runs hither and thither capturing as much excitement as he can. But then he gets "pleasure indigestion." His senses become numb and he doesn't feel the excitement anymore. "Let's go somewhere else," he'll say, "I'm bored with this stuff." I know the feeling also!

This tendency to become immune to pleasure is a significant cause of unhappiness, especially if you don't understand what is happening. The stimulation of our pleasure centers is an essential component in our happiness—indeed, of our very lives. If these centers are not stimulated, we go into deep depression.

Many experiments have been carried out to demonstrate what happens when humans are deprived of all sensory stimulation. It is surprising how rapidly the disorienting effects set in. In one group of experiments, human subjects are subjected to a constant, unchanging environment. All stimulation is kept constant; there is no change in light, temperature, or noise. At first the subject goes to sleep. When he awakens his mind drifts, then after a few hours he begins to hallucinate. At first the images are pleasant, but later they become intensely frightening.

Another experience that provides evidence for our need of stimulation is that associated with dark climates. In northern countries that have long winters with few hours of daylight, a special form of depression is common. It has been linked both to the diminished amount of sunlight as well as to the long hours indoors with little sensory stimulation of the outdoors.

Yes, we need stimulation to keep us normal. But when we are *overstimulated*, our pleasure centers become saturated and dull. We are not able to experience happiness because we cannot enjoy the pleasurable sensations we so desperately seek. We need to have the right balance of pleasurable stimulation to be happy.

THE DISTORTION OF PLEASURE

There's another problem that is increasingly common in our pleasure-hungry society. Not only are we becoming "dulled" to pleasure, but we are increasingly distorting our experience of it.

When we start out in life, very simple things give us pleasure. Slowly we increase our appetite for variety until we expect excitement or pleasure in more sophisticated, often less wholesome forms. We may begin to search for pleasure in the unsavory corners of life. And as we seek pleasure in these "unholy arenas," happiness declines.

Abundant evidence for our tendency to distort pleasure comes to us from the realm of human sexuality.

Sex is an important aspect of existence. Unless we are incapacitated by disease, we spend much of our life in the pursuit of pleasure through our sexuality. It is a major part of everyone's existence and an important aspect of all relationships, even those in which no direct sexual expression takes place.

In our culture, sexuality is probably the most talked-about and oft-pursued pleasure of all. It is hard to find a movie or a television program—or even a commercial!—that doesn't touch on the topic. As a society, we are preoccupied with sex to the point of its becoming a national obsession. Most people (and especially males) think about, talk about, indulge in, and fantasize about sex to the point of excess.

Now, I concede that sex is a necessary, God-ordained, part of life. But when teenagers report feeling "burned out" on sex before age twenty, we clearly have a problem! Years before they are ready to take up their responsibilities as marriage partners, a great many young people have experienced everything there is to experience about their sexuality. And because for them sex occurs outside the context of a committed, intimate, and abiding relationship, their sexual experience lacks depth and cannot satisfy their deep needs.

There is no way a sexually promiscuous lifestyle can bring happiness—we are not made that way. God's laws about sexual control are not the arbitrary killjoy antics of an over-strict parent, but the loving concerns of a Creator who knows what His creation needs to be happy. His boundaries on sex, like His limits on all human indulgences, are for our benefit and protection. God has given us our sexuality as a gift. And when we disfigure its pleasure in human experience by overindulgence and practice outside of marriage, we run the grave risk of robbing this gift of its ability to give real pleasure.

The distortion of sexual pleasure is demonstrated especially clearly in the sexual perversions indulged in by many people today. Many sexual perversions begin, I believe, because early experience of "basic" sex is not found to be enjoyable enough. So a heightened sexual pleasure is sought through associating sexual arousal with the adrenalin arousal that comes with fear or other strong negative emotions. Doing something that others disapprove of adds a certain thrill to the experience. This thrill soon dulls, so new thrills must be sought to add a new high to the experience.

Quickly, the pursuit of some new pleasure in sex moves people to associating other forms of exciting arousal with sexual arousal. Having sex in strange places—or doing anything that is beyond the norm or even "taboo"—adds a new excitement that enhances the sexual excitement. The eventual result is the inability to enjoy basic sexual arousal with the additional forms of excitement.

For some, adding pain to sex creates this additional excitement—and some even go so far as to add the ultimate thrill of death. The alarming truth is that sado-masochistic forms of sexual expression are showing an alarming increase in incidence, as is near-suicide for sexual stimulation. Our society has started down the road of extreme perversity in how it experiences sex—and this is true of other forms of pleasure. Because our pleasure centers quickly become dulled from overstimulation, more and more we are seeking pleasure through practices that can bring nothing but unhappiness.

BACK TO BASICS

But how does this all apply to normal, churchgoing, respectable people? Unfortunately, more than we might think! Almost anyone can get caught up seeking ever-increasing pleasure without realizing just how subtle the process is. In my practice, I find myself spending more and more time teaching my patients to back off from always wanting special thrills. And I am talking about "normal" people—not just "perverts." Ordinary folks can easily get caught up in trying to enhance pleasure by engaging in unhealthy kinds of stimulation.

In the realm of sexuality, for instance, many resort to the use of fantasy or pornography to add new excitement to marital sex. The trouble is that this practice quickly dulls the pleasure centers; it creates an appetite for further exploration and excitement. While some novel experience in sex might be exciting now, it quickly becomes ordinary and you'll keep looking for the next and "better" excitement.

So, how can we avoid falling in the trap of dulling our pleasure centers and requiring more and more stimulation in order to feel pleasure? We must learn how to keep our pleasures simple and "basic."

Be content with ordinary experiences; don't keep looking for new or novel sensations. Exercise control over the temptation to fantasize sexual experiences, and lower your expectations for every experience to be extraordinary. I may be speaking primarily to my male readers at this point, but much old-fashioned fundamental discipline of the eyes and mind is urgently needed in our day and age. And when you become content with ordinary feelings, you will find that they are beautiful in and of themselves, and far more satisfying than thrill-loaded experiences.

This phenomenon (of always seeking new excitement) is not widely recognized, even in Christian circles. It is disappointing to me, for example, that modern Christian sex handbooks do not recognize dangers that may lie in encouraging couples to engage in fantasy or other forms of stimulation to enhance sexual experiences. There is no stopping the pursuit of forbidden pleasures if we don't know how to enjoy the basics. Perversion is subtle and seemingly innocent at first, and even normal people can find themselves well and truly hooked!

I recently counseled with a very fine and deeply spiritual minister who, early in his adolescence, had gotten caught up with masturbating to pornography (a very common practice among youth) and continued this for many years. His guilt after every indulgence was overwhelming, but it only served to make him more obsessed with pornography.

At first he had only used pictures of girls in bathing suits, then he had moved to photography magazines depicting nude models. But these pictures soon lost their ability to arouse him, so he had moved on to low-key pornography and eventually hardcore porn—often having to pay four or five times the face value of a magazine to get it from a friend.

By the time this man was in his early twenties—married, and beginning his ministry—hardcore pornography no longer stimulated him, so he began to go to peep shows and "skin flicks." What finally scared him was when he began to desire the more bizarre pictures of mutilation and sex with children, so he sought therapy.

This man found that sex with his wife was a great disappointment because he had defiled his God-given drive for pleasure through sexuality. He had developed such an obsession with pornography that it was difficult to focus on normal sexual experiences. No doubt we will work in therapy together for a long time to undo the damage of his early sexual distortions. Not until he can find pleasure in ordinary experiences will he be happy again.

REGAINING THE ABILITY TO ENJOY PLEASURE

There is another side to this problem. While some people have overstimulated the pleasure centers to the point that they require more and more stimulation to feel pleasure, others have cut themselves off from any pleasure at all. They cannot "give in" to pleasure, either because they feel too guilty or because they don't believe they deserve it.

Guilt can be a significant obstacle to happiness when it robs us of our ability to experience healthy pleasures. As I have pointed out in a previous chapter, not all feelings of guilt are God's convictions. There is a form of guilt we call "neurotic"—it is "false" because it results not from the conviction of real sin and wrong-doing but from very strict early influences that are internalized as a system of self-punishment. A common form of self-punishment is robbing yourself of the freedom to enjoy something.

To some degree we all have a measure of neurotic guilt—our culture sees to this! It's not even all bad, since some of it helps us to be responsible citizens. When it is experienced to the extent that it destroys our happiness, however, neurotic guilt is a problem we must address.

Some years ago, when we still lived in South Africa, my wife and I invited a newly arrived missionary couple to dinner. Because they were new to our country, we wanted them to feel very special, so we worked hard to make it a memorable evening. The table was set for a candlelight dinner, and we used our best china and silverware.

Throughout the evening the wife of the visiting couple seemed troubled. She only picked at her meal, and she gave many signs that she was not at ease. I drew the husband aside at a convenient moment and asked him what the problem was. He apologized profusely as he told me that his wife suffered from guilt feelings about almost everything, and that these feelings were so intense she could never relax and just enjoy things.

When she bought shoes, he said, she felt guilty for spending money on herself. When she threw stale bread away she felt guilty for wasting food. And on occasions such as this, where she was the center of special attention, she felt overwhelmed by her self-consciousness and guilt. When we understood what the problem was, my wife and I felt very sad for our guest, but we also gave a big sigh of relief—we had begun to feel guilty ourselves for being poor hosts!

Guilt is often legitimate—but when it is not, the destruction it can work in our lives is great. Guilt-ridden people are seldom happy people, because the guilt diminishes their capacity to enjoy ordinary pleasure.

When guilt is real it must be heeded. True guilt, whether it is God's conviction or the response of a healthy conscience, must be acted upon. One should confess it, change whatever needs to be changed, and restore whatever needs restoring. It is then a very healthy emotion that brings healing and wholeness. And not surprisingly, when true guilt is responded to in a responsible way, an enhanced feeling of happiness always follows.

DEVELOPING YOUR PLEASURE CENTER

Life is rich—it holds an abundant smorgasbord of healthy pleasures that can be pursued with gusto. There is *no excuse* to be miserable in this life. If we are, it is because we have chosen to be miserable. We can spend our lives grudgingly keeping ourselves from enjoying legitimate pleasures, or we can free ourselves to be happy.

Some of the greatest pleasure in life can be found in meaningful work. Permanent leisure will never make us really happy, since work is as natural and necessary to life as eating and sleeping. "Wait until I retire," I hear many say in my consulting room, "then I will be free to find something to make me happy." Nonsense! I am convinced that if a study were conducted on the relationship between work and happiness, you would discover that meaningful work always enhances our happiness.

Unfortunately, there are many people who derive little satisfaction from their jobs and must grin and bear their way through a humdrum routine. But this is still no excuse not to find pleasure in many other areas of life. If you enjoy your work, you have a "bonus," but work enjoyment is not absolutely necessary to happiness, for there are many pleasures to be enjoyed outside of what one is called upon to do for a living.

Take *hobbies*, for instance. Being able to complete a creative task, no matter how small, universally produces pleasure. I love teaching people to be creative. Not too long ago I taught my one son-in-law how to rebuild the brakes on his car. Not only did he save money; he also thrilled at the pleasure this accomplishment gave him.

Hobbies do not have to cost money. One can collect bits of nature for nothing. Take wildflowers, for example. On a recent trip to Switzerland, I began to collect samples of wildflowers, pressing each flower between the pages of a book. I brought them home to one of my daughters, who collects them, and she was overjoyed; I could not have purchased a better homecoming present at any price. I now love to reminisce with her over each flower and where it came from.

Friendships, carefully selected and cultivated, can also be a rich source of pleasure, especially when they involve spiritual support and encouragement. Even when friends move away and contact becomes less frequent, they can continue to be a source of happiness through letters, cards, and telephone calls.

Humor is being taken very seriously in psychological research these days as a promoter of both happiness and health. Numerous national conventions of professionals, including anthropologists and sociologists, have been held in the recent past to explore its value, and hospitals are now using "laughter therapy groups" for patients with chronic pain. A recent notice on a bulletin board sums up the whole idea by exhorting, "Jest for the health of it."

Laughter is a great healing force because it maximizes the body's ability to heal itself. Pleasures that provide laughter are the healthiest of all, not only for our bodies and minds, but also for our spiritual growth.

A year or so ago I visited a retreat conducted by a prominent physician who specializes in the treatment of terminally ill cancer patients. I talked with a large number of cancer victims ranging in ages from seventeen to seventy. All had been diagnosed as terminal and been given "last resort" treatments. Now they had gathered at this retreat to learn how to live their last months to the fullest.

What impressed me about this retreat was the laughter. After ten days of sharing and facing the reality of their circumstances, these people had come to the point that they could laugh freely with each other. They were funny and fun-loving, and their humor moved me deeply. Some told me that when they had been in the best of health they had never learned really to laugh at themselves and their problems. Now they could do this with great feeling. And with this new freedom to laugh came a new depth to their faith. They could believe in a new and meaningful way.

With what result? The physician conducting the retreat reports that many of these cancer patients will outlive their short life expectancies. Their immune systems will become stimulated by the pleasure that their laughter encouraged, and they will achieve a new perspective on life. The progress of their disease will be slowed and in some cases even reversed.

The results of this experiment are proving that our minds and bodies do indeed respond to a happy environment, especially a happy internal environment.

HELPFUL THOUGHTS

Here are some suggestions on how to enhance your happiness through the pleasure of laughter:

- Learn from the laughter of children. Play their games, mimic their freedom, and dream their dreams.
- Try not to take yourself too seriously. Laugh at your mistakes and quickly forgive the mistakes of others.
- Develop a playful attitude toward your problems and anxieties. Handle them with humor and lay them aside with laughter.
- Use laughter as a safety valve to keep yourself relaxed and sane.
- Always look for the sunny side of every difficult experience and inject laughter into tense tempers and jangled nerves.
- Always laugh *with* others, never *at* them.
- Meet each day with a sense of humor and determination to enjoy all of its pleasures.
- Invite God to be a part of every smile and pass His happiness on to others. Happiness is like perfume—you can't spray it on others without getting some on yourself.
- Remember the words of Ralph Waldo Emerson:

> To laugh often and much
> To win respect of intelligent people
> and the affection of children;
> To earn the appreciation of honest critics
> and endure the betrayal of false friends;
> to appreciate beauty;
> To find the best in others; . . .
> This is to have succeeded.

Happiness Is Wanting the Right Things

SHORTLY BEFORE KATHLEEN AND I MARRIED in our early twenties, we sat down one evening to talk about our future together. We shared with each other some of our goals and conversed about our dreams. We both tend to be visionaries, and in our fantasy we laid out the plans we had for our life together. We thought that if we were united in our ambitions we would have a much greater chance of achieving them than if we each took off in our own direction. But naturally there were some areas where our dreams were different, so we began to barter and haggle. I wanted this; she wanted that! How could "this" be possible since "this" was in conflict with "that"?

One thing we did agree on from the outset was that God would rule our lives. We were both committed to discerning God's plan for us and being faithful to our walk with Him. We had seen quite a few of our friends fall away from faith in God, and we were determined that it wouldn't happen to us.

"But," I said to Kathleen, "it would be helpful to set down clear objectives that could guide our ambitions. This way we could pull together and be more successful at achieving them." Kathleen agreed, so we started to write out a list of things we wanted in life.

It was a long list! Sure, it contained many *material* things. We wanted a home of our own with a double garage, two cars, and a comprehensive library of books. Kathleen wanted her own typewriter—not just the standard mechanical sort, but one of the new electric ones with a typing ball that zipped across the carriage. I wanted a camping tent (I've always been a Boy Scout at heart). Kathleen wanted a sewing machine.

Our list also contained things we wanted to do. I wanted to learn how to sail. Kathleen wanted to crochet. I wanted to fly. She wanted to learn how to tailor her own clothes. I wanted to see the world. She wanted to learn how to be a writer. As I said, it was a long list!

Our list also contained *nonmaterial* desires. We wanted at least two children (we stopped at three). We desired to be good parents and longed that our children would grow up faithful to the gospel we loved. We wanted to find a way to serve our Lord in some form of Christian ministry.

When we were through with our list, we packed it away, and as time passed we forgot about it. Then, on the occasion of our thirtieth wedding anniversary, we remembered the list we had made so many years before. Along the way we had lost the original document, so just for the heck of it we sat down together to see if we could reconstruct it from memory.

As we recalled all the things we had wanted out of life in our early twenties, we made an amazing discovery. Over the years, God, in His faithfulness, had given us every single item we can remember on our list. Oh, perhaps there were a few petty items we had not received or accomplished, but we honestly could not recall what they were. Everything that had mattered was ours!

"Why is it," we asked ourselves as we sat together eating our anniversary dinner, "that we have achieved all we set out to achieve, with lots of time to spare? Were we not ambitious enough? Did we not dream big enough?"

As we thought about it, we both concluded that the answer was quite simple: *We had desired the right things* — "right" in the sense that they did not violate any of God's plans for our lives. Now, obviously, some of what we had wanted was selfish and possibly influenced by our materialistic world view, but God had granted us a few of our immature desires nevertheless. Also, there had been some disappointments, and we did not always get what we wanted when we wanted it. But overall we felt very privileged, almost as if God had "spoiled" us.

This brought home to me a very important life lesson. We all want certain things from life. But we are not going to get all we want unless we want the "right" things. And we can only know what these "right" things are if we have a clear conscience before God and seek to do His bidding. This is the clear message of 1 John 3:21–22:

> But dearly loved friends, if our consciences are clear, we can come to the Lord with perfect assurance and trust, and get whatever we ask for because we are obeying him and doing the things that please him (LB).

St. Augustine puts it all in a nutshell: "Happy is the man [and woman] who, in the course of a complete life, has everything he desires, provided he desires nothing amiss."

Happiness comes from wanting the right things in life. It is the consequence of deliberately creating the right appetites.

REVIEWING OUR APPETITES

We all have appetites, and not just for food. We want so many things in life—nice clothes, perhaps, or a good job, exotic foods, education at the best institutions, or membership in the most exclusive clubs. And the marvelous thing about our world is that if we are willing to work hard enough for it, we can have almost everything our hearts desire. But if we desire wrongly we can easily end up miserable. Also, if you can't be satisfied with what you have, you'll never be happy with what you have yet to get. Psalms 106:15 has a very solemn warning we don't heed often enough: "And he gave them their request; but sent leanness into their soul."

You may want to read this psalm for yourself. It tells of Israel's rebelliousness—how the people lusted in the wilderness and tempted God in the desert. They kept asking for things that weren't right. Finally God gave in to them, and they discovered that getting what they wanted didn't bring them the peace and satisfaction they needed.

Our appetites, therefore, can shape our expectations and even our characters. We become what we desire. We are shaped toward what we so desperately seek in life.

How do we form our appetites so that they are healthy? How do we direct our desires so that they are consistent with the good things of life? These questions are not only important to securing our happiness, but extremely necessary in learning how to discern God's plan for our lives.

My wife and I are now looking at the next stage of our life together. Our children are grown up, and we are beginning the grandparenting stage. Once again we are trying to unite our desires into some common goals. To want the wrong things for this stage, whether we get them or not, is to court disaster in terms of our happiness. So how are we determining what the "right" things are?

There are three steps that have been very helpful to us. Follow with me as I walk you through them, and perhaps they will help you maintain some balance to your appetites. The three steps I will discuss are:

- Review your values,
- Revise your desires, and
- Relish the right things.

REVIEW YOUR VALUES

At every stage of your life, it's helpful to do a little exercise in clarifying your values. At very least, one should do this in adolescence, early adulthood, during the parenting stage, and again after middle age. Values clarification is important because it helps make you aware of what you seek in life. Most people have no sense of what their values are. They don't know what is important to them. They have no idea what drives them. They don't think about how they value money, religion, friendships, or success. Deeply embedded in their beliefs and attitudes are the values they attach to objects or principles, yet they are oblivious to these values, hardly giving them a thought!

Now, whether you are consciously aware of them or not, values influence what you do and how you feel. They determine *where* you go, *what* you buy, and *when* you start a project or quit it. They are the indicators of those things you truly desire in life.

Psychologists rightly attach great importance to the benefits of knowing what your values are, in having a very clear understanding of what drives you. Sometimes these values can be in conflict with each other and be the source of much unhappiness. At other times they can cause you to want the wrong things in life—things that cannot make you happy.

Living in Southern California has exposed us to a number of tragedies in the past few years. We have been near the scene of a major airplane crash, several floods, numerous landslides, and a couple of serial murders. Then, not too long ago, a major fire devastated one hundred eighty houses near our home. The fire ripped through a very wealthy neighborhood, and at first as I watched the TV news broadcasts I did not experience much sympathy—the VIP names mentioned gave me the impression that the monetary value of what was lost could be easily replaced. But as the cameras took us through the ashes, we saw the remains of a pet that was greatly loved and a scorched child's toy left behind in the scurry to safety. My heart softened, and I understood the pain of such a catastrophe.

I also began to think! Suppose *my* home was on fire and everything I possess—money, friends, children, computers, hobbies, and the rest—were in the house. What if a fireman said to me, "You've got thirty seconds to go in and collect whatever you want"? What would I fetch to safety?

It was a very sobering thought, and it caused me to review the value I attach to everything I possess. Thinking "What would I rescue in a fire?" is a classic exercise for values.

Or here's another: Suppose you have to undergo surgery for a brain tumor and the surgeon says, "I can operate in a number of different ways, but each way means damage will be done to some function and loss. You can make the choice—would you rather lose your sight, hearing, intelligence, walking ability, emotional stability, or sense of touch?"

How do you react? Which function would you surrender so that the others may be preserved?

These are sobering exercises because they point up the importance we attach to the various elements in our lives. These are our *values*, and they have a powerful influence over us, even if we don't think about them. Often, it takes a catastrophe to bring them into our awareness.

VALUES CLARIFICATION EXERCISE

Here's a more thorough exercise for reviewing your values prior to taking the next two steps: Take a few blank sheets of paper so that you can review your values. Write down on the first sheet a list of the common things most people desire in life—things like money, title, prestige, security, power, status, love, appearance, self-esteem, respect, and so forth! Add your own desires to this list. Then alongside each of these "things," rate the value you attach to it on a scale from 0 to 10, where 0 is "no value" and 10 is "extremely high value." (A 5 would be a moderate value.)

Now, take a second sheet of paper and answer each of the following questions as honestly as you can:

- What is *important* to me in life?
- What do I *prize* more than anything else?
- What do I *seek* more than anything else?

- Where do I *spend* most of my time?
- Where do I *desire to be* more than anywhere else?

Set these answers aside for the moment. We will examine your responses in the next section.

How do we know what is *good* for us and what is *bad?* How can we tell if something we want is right, or if obtaining it will make us happy? There are no easy answers to these questions. The truth lies finally in whether it is something God wants us to have or not.

There are, of course, some things that according to Scripture are clearly *bad* for us. For instance, to want to take revenge on someone who has hurt us or to desire that someone else fail just so that we can feel better are not to be part of a Christian's goals. There are also universally *good* desires. To want to be a more honest and loving person, have a more congenial personality, or build strength of character are good in anyone's book, including God's! They can be placed without hesitation on our list of things to achieve because God has already declared them as being *right* for all of us. The rest need to be prayed about carefully, so that you can discern whether they are good for you or not.

REVISE YOUR DESIRES

The desires of our heart are unique to each one of us. Like a fingerprint, each person's "value profile" is unique. But some values are better than other values. And unlike our fingerprints, the pattern of desires, which determine who we are, *can be changed.* This is the message of the gospel. Romans 12:2 is most encouraging: "And be not conformed to this world: but be ye transformed by the renewing of your mind, that ye may prove what is that good, and acceptable, and perfect, will of God."

We can dramatically transform the desires of our hearts by presenting ourselves as living sacrifices to God (v. 1). You do not have to

copy the behavior and customs of this world, but be a new and different person with a fresh newness in all you do and think. Then you will learn from your own experience how his ways will really satisfy you (v. 2, LB).

This scripture reads almost like a handbook on personal growth!

We *can* change our desires so that they conform to what God wants for us. Take each of the items you listed in the previous section and the values you attached to them, then pray over each one, asking God to help you place His value on each item. Next to each of the values you had previously given, write down what you think God's value for it is. Write it in red ink so it stands out. Now pray that God will help you bring your values into line with His.

Take the second sheet of paper from the previous exercise and pray over each answer there, again asking the question, "Is this what God wants from me?" If your answer is "no," then write down what you believe God does desire of you.

An exercise such as this, if prayerfully undertaken, can revolutionize your value structure and put you more in touch with yourself. Not only must we correct those values that are undesirable, but we also need to live in greater harmony with those values we consider right. A clear understanding of our values will affect the way we make decisions and help us to grow and change in ways that will produce a greater level of happiness.

RELISH THE RIGHT THINGS

We need to pray constantly for a greater appetite for "right" things. Our desires can be shaped by conscious thoughts that review and relish what we believe to be God's wishes for us.

One of the greatest value conflicts between what our culture teaches and the message of the gospel is over the issue of *riches*. If we are going to miss happiness because we desire the wrong things in life, we will be more likely to do so in the realm of money than anywhere else.

Most values that have to do with money have the potential to become distorted, unless we prayerfully guard them. Whenever money is involved we seem to get our values out of balance. We seem either to want it too much or too feel disproportionate guilt over what we have!

The financial demands of modern life are enormous, and most of us never seem to have enough of this world's wealth. We desire to give our children a better education, better health, and a better start in life than our parents gave us. And it all costs money!

Money is a necessary evil even for the work of the gospel. I am on the board of a large mission organization—and we constantly struggle for enough money to carry out evangelism in those parts of the world that need it. Without money our churches cannot carry out their work of reaching the unsaved and helping the needy.

So how can we place our desire for money in proper perspective? First, let us again remind ourselves that money is neutral. It neither determines nor destroys our happiness in and of itself. What counts is *what* and *how* we desire it and what we *do* with it. And this is where our values come in.

Jesus deals with this issue very specifically in the Sermon on the Mount. Matthew 6:19 reads, "Do not store up for yourselves treasure on earth, where it grows rusty and moth-eaten, and thieves break in and steal" (NEB).

Why? The answer goes right to the core of the issue. "For where your treasure is, there will your heart be also" (v. 21, NEB).

No issue concerning money can be clearer. It is in the value or the meaning we attach to money that its joy or despair arises. If you value money with *all* your heart, you will be miserable. If you value money as a tool to be used creatively, both in your life and in God's service, your money can bring you great happiness.

WHERE IS YOUR HEART?

As I watched the TV news reports of the fires that swept through that prestigious neighborhood of Los Angeles, I visualized the residents returning to the ashes of their homes. Where would they go first? Where would I go first if I were in their shoes? I imagined a daughter running straight to a stable to grieve over her beloved horse, or perhaps a son running to the remains of his stereo collection. (Who would go for the safe or security box?) Again, I asked myself: "Where would I go?" "Where does anyone go?" The answer is not difficult to discern! You go to where your heart is, because your heart is always centered on what you value most.

It is both comforting and disconcerting to realize that Jesus knows exactly where we would go. When He preached the Sermon on the Mount, there were no banks, no safety deposit boxes, no locks, no plastic bags. Whatever you stored was vulnerable to thieves, moths, and rust. And despite all our modern security devices, this is still true. Everything we value in this life is easily lost unless our values are centered on the ultimate of that which is "right" to desire—eternal things.

HELPFUL THOUGHTS

Where Is Your Heart?

- Is it locked in your safe deposit box, kept secure and impenetrable to hurts?
- Is it in a faraway land, seeking a fortune away from the love your family needs?
- Is it preoccupied with comfort and pleasure-seeking, missing the real joys of life?
- Is it living a whole life, balancing its own needs against the needs of a hungry world?
- Is it developing the habit of always dreaming the right things and desiring nothing amiss?
- Is it seeking to place the priority of eternity over the temporary benefits of the present?
- What does it treasure *above* everything else?

Remember, "Where your treasure is, there will your heart be also."

PRINCIPLE TWELVE

Happiness Is Something You Learn

I ONCE HEARD A STORY about a carding mill that, in the days before electricity, used an old, blind horse to provide motive power. Hour after hour, day after day, week after week, this horse walked in a circle about thirty feet in diameter, pulling a pole that drove the mill. Round and round it walked, earning its keep.

In the evenings and on weekends, the horse was turned loose in a pasture close by to graze. And in that pasture, worn into the grass, were several large circles about thirty feet across. That horse had walked so long in a fixed circle that even when let free in a large field it continued to walk and graze in the same circle.

Not only are blind horses creatures of habit; we are, too. Habits are important to all of us. We prefer routine, and we function best when we get into a routine of behaviors that have predictable outcomes.

Another thing about habits: they are relatively easy to learn but hard to break. And this goes especially for bad habits; they often seem to linger with us despite our best intentions. Every New Year, millions prove that this is true. Even the apostle Paul struggled with this reality of his basic nature: "When I want to do good, I don't; and when I try not to do wrong, I do it anyway." (Rom. 7:19, LB).

Now the point I want to stress here is that happiness is a habit we can learn—a way of approaching life that eventually becomes routine. Fortunate circumstances or a genetic tendency to cheerfulness may help, but are not essential. Much more important is disciplined choice—deliberately and consistently choosing those attitudes and actions that will lead to happiness. In a way, all the other chapters of this book are intended to show various ways you can develop the habit of happiness.

If happiness is a habit, however, so is *un*happiness. That means that if we are to be happy we must not only learn the happiness habit, but also unlearn many habits that produce unhappiness.

UNHAPPINESS AS A HABIT

Let's begin by considering how unhappiness can be learned. Some psychologists have proposed the idea that early in life, due to various influences, we develop a "life-script." It's as if someone else has written a play for our lives, determining how we should make decisions or react to circumstances.

According to this theory, people live out a sort of plan for their lives in which the determining factors are the habits and beliefs they have learned. This plan contains all the prerequisites that determine what will happen to us. And it originates early in life, set there by the people who have the most influence over us.

It is an interesting concept, provided we don't take the deterministic aspect of it too far. I think its validity lies in the fact that we are creatures of habit. Once we learn to think or behave in a certain way, we tend to continue behaving or thinking that way.

For instance, if a person comes to think of himself as a failure, then he will continue to think of himself as a failure, and this belief will probably set him up to fail many times. So in a sense, such a person can be said to have a "failure" life-script—a set of habits that predisposes him to failure and therefore to unhappiness.

Another person might have a "scapegoat" life-script, which causes her to always take the blame for something that goes wrong. Early in life, this person might have been the one everyone else in the family "dumped on," the one who was blamed whenever anything was broken or missing. "Scapegoats" grow up believing that they do in fact cause things to go wrong, that they are the "jinx" that attracts bad luck. By continually accepting the blame for every misfortune, they create an unhappiness habit for themselves.

Many other fascinating but unhealthy life-scripts have been identified and labeled. There is the "hero"—the one who always jumps forward to rescue someone else, often then bringing condemnation upon themselves. For women there is the "Mother Hubbard" script, in which the woman spends her life nurturing and taking care of everyone but herself, or the "poor little me" script, in which she habitually plays the role of a victim looking for a rescuer. For men there are scripts like "Big Daddy"—with an exaggerated idea of what it means to be a responsible father and husband—and "Playboy"—the man who spends his life chasing after the "perfect woman" who doesn't exist.

Let me once again stress that what lies behind these unhealthy scripts is a *pattern of habits* that combine to produce unhappiness. Patterns like these are established early in life, and we must continue to work throughout life to counteract them. While it may help a lot just to be aware of an unhappy life-script, professional counseling may be required to undo their domination.

EMOTIONAL BAD HABITS

In addition to unhealthy life-scripts, certain emotional bad habits can also produce unhappiness.

For instance, it has been well established through psychological research that negative and destructive emotions such as anger, fear, and disgust are biologically much stronger than the positive emotions of happiness and love. In other words, when we are angry or fearful, these emotions dominate our moods and create very powerful and pervasive changes in our hormone levels, blood pressure, and muscular tension—changes that can displace our happiness. In order to be happy, therefore, we must learn to dispose of these negative emotions as quickly as possible.

We can even take it a step further and say that happiness emerges naturally when there is little or no anger and fear present. Most people are happy unless something makes them sad. Remove the sadness and people naturally revert to being happy.

It's like sunshine. The sun will shine if there are no clouds. Similarly, if the clouds of anger and fear are removed, happy emotions appear spontaneously. All we need to be happy, then, is to remove the bad emotional habits that have crept in during the many years of our lives.

Happiness is not an emotion that can be "forced." It cannot be conjured up whenever it is desired. If happiness is to be real, it must be allowed to emerge as a normal reaction to the right stimuli. The point at which we *can* control and create our happiness is the point of removing negative emotional habits that are serving as obstacles, so that our natural feelings of well-being can emerge.

It is worth your while, therefore, to try to create a positive, happy atmosphere around you. Being friendly and bringing out the best in others will increase your own happiness. So will practicing forgiveness, disposing of your anger as soon as possible, and minimizing your fears by daring to confront the things that threaten you. Put a little extra effort into making your life circumstances as free as possible from anger and fear, and a happier atmosphere will emerge.

HAPPINESS AS A HABIT OF MENTAL AND SPIRITUAL HEALTH

Happiness correlates positively with mental health. Anything you can do to become psychologically healthier will contribute to good feelings and thus to your happiness. Conversely, getting involved in unnecessary conflict is bound to lead to unhappiness.

I would also say that happiness correlates with a healthy spirituality. Psychological health is one of the payoffs for a closer walk with God. Everything about the Christian gospel is healthy and produces both spiritual and psychological renewal.

Sure, there are those who distort the gospel. They inculcate excessive and inappropriate guilt feelings; they preach distorted values about success and material wealth; and they manipulate their followers through misused power.

But the gospel itself remains pure and unadulterated. And when it does its work without human misinterpretation and under the direction of God the Holy Spirit, it is both agreeable and healthy. It does not create anger, but helps us resolve our hurts and forgive our enemies. It does not foster fear, but instills courage to face all of life's threats and challenges. It certainly is not designed to nourish unhappiness, but rather to nurture joy and gladness, the emotions of eternity.

If you are not experiencing the full fruits of the gospel, then perhaps you need to examine your heart and mind, making sure you believe a "pure" gospel and seeking to uproot any emotional "bad habits" that are getting in the way.

Here is a brief checklist for you to take stock of your negative emotions:

- Do you find that you are full of hate?
- Do you blame others for your unhappiness?
- Do you pout whenever you can't get your way?
- Do you find that you envy the gifts or blessings of others?
- Are you very sensitive so that you are easily hurt?
- Do you hold grudges?

- Are you unforgiving, preferring to repay others for the hurt they cause you?
- Are you full of fears and uncertain how to handle them?

The more of these questions you answer with "yes"—or even "maybe"—the more likely it is that you are dominated by emotional bad habits and need to do some changing.

CORRECTING YOUR INHIBITIONS

It is very easy to learn these habits of the mind that obstruct happiness. The mind is the servant of our thoughts, and the body is the servant of the mind. Our thoughts shape and mold our minds, forming deep habits, and our bodies will obey the operation of these habits.

I am not talking here about "mind over matter" or any esoteric New Age phenomena. I am simply pointing out that our thinking controls how we feel and behave. It is just a matter of fact. Our bodies react to what goes on in our minds in a very straightforward "cause and effect" pattern. If I think angry thoughts, my body will react by going into an attack mode. If I think fear, my body will adopt the appropriate fear response.

These "bad habits" of the mind can, therefore, have devastating impact throughout our whole being. Weak, fearful, helpless thoughts break us down. Strong, pure, happy thoughts help build the body in vitality and grace. The thoughts we need to concentrate on, therefore, are those that are healthy. We must turn them into habits.

What we learn in early childhood can set the stage for later happiness or unhappiness. Unfortunately, some children have unhappy parents who can easily reproduce patterns of pain in their offspring. They set up prohibitions and requirements that give a clear message: "You must not be happy."

Now, such parents don't consciously set out to make their kids miserable. But the impact of their training and their relationship with their children is to set up habits of unhappiness that can stay with the children all of their lives.

I recently had to confront a couple with just such a pattern in their parenting. I forced them to stand back and see what they were doing to their son. At eleven years of age he was becoming an old man. He was being pressured to perform at school way beyond what he was capable of doing.

Home was a concentration camp! "Concentrate on your studies" was the most frequent phrase that rang through the house. Instead of accepting their son's limitations, the parents were pushing him as hard as they could. "You'll never amount to anything unless you are top of your class. Work longer! We want better grades!" they demanded. They withheld all childhood pleasures, and they made the most bizarre threats of what would happen if the boy did not deliver a scholastic performance that was up to their standards.

Only when their son finally plunged into a deep depression did these parents wake up to the harm they were causing him, and I fear we may never completely undo this harm.

There was never any question that these parents loved their son. But in their perfectionistic demands and their neglect of many important aspects in a child's life, they were making it extremely unlikely that their son would ever be happy in life. They were teaching him all the basic rules for unhappiness:

- Always try to do more than can reasonably be expected—so you frequently fail.
- Always condemn yourself for your failure—so you always feel inadequate.
- Always punish your failure by becoming miserable and depressed.

It works every time! These are the perfect prescriptions for unhappiness.

Psychologists describe the demands of parents such as these as "injunctions." Injunctions in fairy-tale language are "curses." They go something like this: "If you do _____, then _____ will happen." They are warnings and condemnations that usually are quite arbitrary—and they may be stated directly or merely implied. They reflect the fears, wishes, anger, and desires of the parent or parents. When used excessively, they become deeply entrenched in the mind of a child, so well learned that even in old age they still have the power to control the happiness or unhappiness of the unfortunate victim.

Some injunctions that parents inculcate are relatively minor: "Don't make noise; your father will wake up and spank you," or "Don't laugh so loudly, you'll annoy the neighbors." Others are more serious, like "You have no right to be happy when we are sad" or "There's something wrong with people who enjoy sex."

Minor or major, these injunctions become habits of the heart and mind and have the potential to destroy happiness. They are often coupled with disapproval and withdrawal of love by parents who are zealous to bring their children up perfectly. This can have the effect of destroying self-respect, robbing the child of initiative, creating a fear of risk-taking, and engendering self-hate. A child who has absorbed a lot of parental injunctions may later spend many years in psychotherapy trying to undo the damage that otherwise well-meaning parents have caused.

Injunctions are "curses" we don't need. And my sad observation as a Christian psychotherapist is that well-intentioned Christian parents are often the greatest culprits. We are overly concerned that our children won't turn out right, so we bombard them with injunctions.

"If you're not a good boy, God will punish you." Poor child! He will have great difficulty later in life trying to undo this fear and come to love such a God. There is much destructive teaching within devout Christian circles about how children should be reared, and each generation of parents passes this misinformation on to the next generation. It's no wonder, then, that the sins and neuroticisms of the parents get passed on to the children of succeeding generations (Exod. 34:7).

BUILDING THE HAPPINESS HABIT

I'll say it once again: *Happiness is something you learn.* The attitudes and behaviors that produce it need to be carefully cultivated and nurtured throughout life.

We begin to build these habits, good or bad, when we are still very young. (And parents can do a lot toward fostering them in their children.) Ideally we need to learn the value of forgiveness and be taught right behaviors with love and respect. We need to continue to build these habits when we are adolescents, especially as we struggle with crazy hormonal changes that often produce sadness and confusion. We then need to reinforce these habits throughout adulthood, even into our senior years. We need happiness in a special way when we reach old age and see life beginning to ebb.

Happiness is a life-script we have to write for ourselves after we have undone the unhappiness scripts and injunctions that were previously formed in our minds. We must break the spell of any "curses" laid on us (figuratively speaking) and determine to be happy whatever our background or life history.

We have to plan for happiness; it doesn't come about automatically. We need to prepare for it with as much care as we would plan a career, a physical development program, or a new business.

The words of the apostle Paul in Philippians 4:11 have helped me tremendously as I have sought to build the happiness habit in my own life: "Not that I speak in respect of want; for I have learned in whatsoever state I am, therewith to be content."

There are three key phrases here: "learned," "whatsoever state," and "content." Do you think Paul knew what he was talking about? As he penned those words, he was chained to a Roman soldier in the emperor Nero's prison. He had just been flogged one hundred ninety-nine strokes, and he was well-aware that his life was near its end. There was no hope of freedom—this was it! Yet he was able to write, "I have learned . . . to be content."

In contrast, as Paul penned those words, Nero was in his palace, full of pomp and glory. We are told that his hallways were made of marble and nearly a mile long. His mules were shod with silver, and he had so many garments he never wore them more than once. But history also records that Nero was a miserable wretch of a man—far from being happy.

The lesson is clear: You can learn to be happy in whatever circumstance you find yourself—with a strong emphasis on the word "learn." It is very easy to be miserable in painful circumstances. Anger at life and resentment toward life's hurts are natural reactions; they do not have to be learned. People automatically identify more with the bad things of life than with the good things. Our lower natures have an easy rapport with pain and wretchedness. Privation and anguish find ready and willing partners in nearly all of us.

It takes courage and determination to say no to self-pity and to rise above the false delights of depression, saying, "I will learn how to be happy, even in these unfortunate circumstances."

What are some of the happiness-producing emotions or habits we can develop? Allow me to suggest a few:

- *Live a relatively disciplined life.* Build in clear directions and develop the habit of completing tasks begun.
- *Try to be loving to most people you know.* You don't have to like them, just love them.
- *Keep your expectations, both for yourself and others, reasonable and within reach.* Build in as many "bonuses" as possible.
- *Share your pains and sorrows with someone else.* You cannot

survive unless you open your heart to others for the comfort they can give. To bear it alone is to be unhappy beyond words.

- *Laugh at your mistakes.* Try not to take yourself too seriously. Laughing at your errors keeps you growing by showing you where to change.
- *Free yourself from any tendency to panic* or to react anxiously to change. Remind yourself that God is in control and that you can trust Him totally.
- *Control your temper and talk about your hurts calmly and clearly.* Teach yourself to keep short accounts and quickly clear the air of grudges.
- *Build tolerance for frustrations.* Delays, or people who block your goals, are a fact of life. The more patience you have, the happier you will be.

THE ROLE OF SADNESS

Now, don't take my point about learning to be happy too far. There are times when it is healthier to be sad than happy, better to be down than up! There are not many such times, but there are some.

Sadness has a very important role to play in our spiritual and psychological health, especially if we have suffered a loss of some sort. It helps us grieve and frees us from the things we cling to.

This past week I counseled with a pastor who has suffered many devastating life-blows over this past year. First he was fired from his church position because of a personality conflict with a senior church official. Then he was involved in a head-on car crash that nearly killed his wife. His sixteen-year-old daughter ran away with a drug addict and hasn't been seen for weeks. Then, to crown it all, he was diagnosed as having a painful disease that is difficult to cure.

This unfortunate pastor, when I first met him in my office, was desperately trying to maintain a brave face. He believed he had to be strong for the sake of his wife and the rest of the family, so he downplayed his misfortune and tried to be cheerful.

What's wrong with this? It's hypocritical, that's what! Playing out a lie brings health neither to spirit or psyche.

It is one thing to rise above your circumstances once you have faced them and to put on a brave face because you have chosen happiness rather than self-pity. It is quite a different matter to ignore or deny real pain and to fool yourself into believing all is well. Because this pastor continued to engage in denial, he became sicker and sicker. The more he refused to face the reality of his life circumstances, the more pain he felt. Finally his body and mind began to rebel, and he broke out with vague, diffuse, and irritating sensations all over his body.

If we are to learn how to be happy, we must begin by being honest—honest with our feelings, honest with how we see life, and honest with how we behave. Sometimes this means we must allow ourselves to be sad or depressed for an appropriate amount of time.

The pastor I was counseling finally began to face the reality of his feelings. While this provoked a profound depression, he quickly recovered and became a tower of strength to his family. But this happened only after he faced his feelings honestly. Any other approach only short-circuits the healing process.

HELPFUL THOUGHTS

What are some of the other ways in which we can "learn" the habit of happiness? Here are some helpful thoughts you can apply to your life as you seek to build better habits for your mind and heart:

- Review the checklist of negative emotional habits I mentioned earlier in this chapter. Take each bad habit that you identified in yourself and pray for God to take care of it by teaching you how to control or remove it.
- Review the checklist of happiness-producing emotions. Take each happy habit you recognize in yourself and pray that God will help you increase your experience with it. If you cannot see any "happy habits" in yourself, pray for wisdom to develop them.
- Reflect on your "life-script" and the "injunctions" you have internalized from your parents, your early friends, and other influences. Write down a strategy for how you might change these scripts or injunctions.
- If you feel that your unhappiness habits are out of control, take the following steps to correct them:
  (1) *Don't retreat any further*. Mark time and try to regroup. Don't make rash decisions at this point; simply try to face up to your unhappiness.
  (2) *Make contact with someone you can talk to.* We cannot always see our problems clearly if we keep them in our

heads. Talking them over with someone else can help give us perspective and clarify what our actions should be.

(3) *Design a clear plan of action.* With the help of the person you have shared with, design a simple "1-2-3" set of steps and follow through on them. Every problem situation has a solution, although it may not be a pleasant or happy one. There *is* an answer to your dilemma.

(4) *Avoid alcohol and sedatives.* These will never solve an unhappiness problem. You need a clear head and keen mind to act responsibly. Drugs and alcohol only temporarily blot out your awareness of your problems.

(5) *Seek psychotherapy or competent counseling.* Severe cases of unhappiness are the product of deeply rooted, learned bad habits. A trained professional may be needed to help you sift through the rubble of your muddled mind and build a new store of peace and joy that once was yours. Don't be afraid to admit you need help, and never look at needing help as a sign of weakness. It takes maturity to admit that you cannot go it alone, and cowards don't have the guts for real maturity!

Happiness Is Developing Close Relationships

THERE IS LITTLE disagreement among researchers on what produces happy people; they seem to agree about almost everything. Above all, however, there is very strong agreement that happiness is produced by having close relationships, especially friends on whom one can depend. The unhappiest people of all are those who have no friends.

It is human nature that one can never be deeply and abidingly happy until we give ourselves in love to others. As we sow the seeds of love we reap the joy of a rich happiness harvest.

Down through the years, Kathleen and I have been blessed to have had many friends in many places. It seems as if it is only when you move on that you really come to value the friendships you leave behind.

In 1971, we came to the United States from South Africa for a year to study and to reorganize our lives. I had already completed my doctorate in psychology and started a clinical practice, but was uncertain about what my future would be, what God was calling me to do. During the year that we spent at the Graduate School of Psychology of Fuller Theological Seminary, Kathleen and I met another couple who were also in transition, and we became close friends. We were alone in a foreign country, suffering from culture shock, and isolated from the rest of our family and friends in South Africa. Our friends, who were from another state, were also far from home, so they took us into their hearts and home.

As the year of our stay drew to a close, we realized we had put down very deep roots of friendship and wondered how we were going to handle the impending separation. We were torn between wanting to stay with our new friends and returning to our old friendships at home.

Just before we were to leave Los Angeles and return to our

homeland, possibly never to return again to the United States, my
wife received a letter from the wife of the other couple. It cap-
tures so beautifully the meaning of a fine friendship that I have
asked my wife's permission to share a little of it with you. It was
written as an "Ode to a Friend," and I think it expresses the
universal meaning of all friendships:

My dear Kathy,

Some friendships mature slowly,
And one day it is suddenly realized that friendship exists.
Ah, how much is wasted in such slowness.

Other friendships are known from the start,
And no time is spent in nursing thoughts for fear of offending;
In mincing words for dread of misunderstanding;
Or in idle wondering—In what are her interests?

Somehow, two minds draw back their encasements before each
    other,
And they see, and they know
That what would be said may be said without hesitation,
And what is thought can be thought openly in loving
    acceptance. . . .

The light of friendship is not constant, neither in one nor the other,
But its shaded corners are not feared nor shunned;
For it proves that today's shadow is tomorrow's beacon.
Therein lies the beauty of two souls, two minds. . . .

Each with its own flickering candle,
Not disturbed that they are from different candleshops,
Or that they were lighted by different matches,
For, after all, all light ultimately has One Source.

Soon, my friend, we must part for some unknown time,
But our friendship will not change!
In full bloom it began.
In full bloom it shall remain.

There are some things not controlled by the natural process of
    birth, growth, and finally death.
Our friendship—Yes, I dare say Love—is such a thing.
It was not born;
It was handed to us full grown by God.
It shall not die,
It will be given back to Him through our lives.

                                    With lasting affection,
                                    Jean

Do you value your friendships? Do you cultivate and nurture them with respect and love? Do you give more than you receive and encourage more than you criticize? Do you have the freedom to be yourself and give this privilege to your friends also? Are you a source of refuge and understanding to others, constantly praying for their welfare? If you are, you are indeed a happy person, because you are building real and abiding friendships.

THE PURPOSE OF FRIENDSHIP

We talk a lot about the value of friendships and close relationships, but what does friendship *do* for us? Why do we *need* intimate relationships? Surprisingly, little has been written about this in psychological literature; more attention has focused on the benefits of friendship than on the purpose it serves.

Setting aside the sexual needs that often form the initial basis for a courting or marital relationship, true friendship—including the deep friendship that should emerge in the marital relationship—serves a number of important purposes.

First of all, it "completes" who we are. We were designed to be creatures of togetherness who need to "enter into relationship." In a sense, we are incomplete in and of ourselves. We need "confirmation," as Martin Buber describes it, and we receive this confirmation in our intimate relationships. The idea that we can be totally self-sufficient, with no need for others, is a myth.

It's true, I suppose, that animals do not need friendships as we do. Yet I wonder, at times, when I observe the devotion of pets to their owners or of pets to each other, whether the need for friendship doesn't extend all the way down to lowly animals. Friends of ours recently "put down" one of their two identical dogs. The dogs had been litter mates and had grown up to be inseparable. After twelve years of closeness, one developed cancer and had to be put to sleep. The remaining dog, almost four months after the separation, is still pining. Every now and then it runs to familiar play spots or brings a bone or plaything into the family room, hoping to encounter his buddy. After a few minutes of searching he slinks to a corner and mopes. It brings tears to my eyes to think of the faithfulness that even animals can have to another animal or to a beloved owner. How much more closeness are we humans capable of?

Naturally, our first need is to be "completed" in relationship with our Maker, but our need for relationship does not stop there. We enter into relationship with other people so as to complete the cycle for ourselves and to provide completeness for them also. Only in this way can we be happy.

Second, relationships help us understand ourselves better by serving as "mirrors" to our souls. We are a mystery to ourselves, are we not? We never really come to know ourselves so clearly that we feel we are in complete control of all behaviors or emotions. We need as much self-understanding as we can tolerate, and the best route to this is through our interaction with friends at a deep and honest level. Relationships that do not move us to a greater level of maturity through self-awareness are really not of much value. Since we are all basically afraid of who we are, we need companions to encourage us in our deeper explorations of self. Intimate sharing helps us drop our facades and gradually remove the inner defenses that protect us from really knowing ourselves. This moves us to greater maturity, healthiness, and happiness.

Third, relationships serve to support us when we feel insecure and assure us in our uncertainties. Life can be a big puzzle. Often you feel all alone and adrift on a sea of confusion. What should we do? Where should we go? How will we survive? Friendships help us answer these questions. True friends provide listening ears so we can share our fears and concerns. Instead of giving a lot of advice, they help us listen to ourselves and find solutions to our questions. If nothing else, they help us keep our perspective straight and place our suffering in the context of what others are experiencing. Comfort comes from knowing that we are not alone; there is always someone who will "be there" for us.

Fourth, relationships provide healing, both spiritual and psychological. Spiritual healing and maturity is fostered by those who encourage and affirm us and by those who tutor us in the ways of God. Psychological healing is aided by the laughter and the tears that all good relationships offer. When you feel bruised and beaten, misunderstood and rejected, a true friend is like an oasis in a parched desert.

True friendship means that there is someone beside you who cares. Yes, we know that God is always there and that He cares, but this presence and caring are especially meaningful and helpful when He is embodied in another person. We all need such friendships.

An anonymous poet captured this aspect of friendship well when he or she wrote:

Oh, this world is not all sunshine—
As the pain of many disclose;
There's a cross for every joy-bell
An' a thorn for every rose;
But the cross is not so greivous
nor the thorn the rosebud wears—
An' the clouds have silver linin's
When someone really cares,

It will send a thrill of rapture
through the framework of the heart,
It will stir the inner being
Till the teardrops want to start;
For this life is worth the livin'
when someone your sorrow shares;
Life is truly worth the livin'
When you know that someone cares.

Anonymous

It is sad that in our day psychotherapists often have to fulfill the role of "friend" to so many. I cannot tell you how often a patient will say to me, "I thank God that you are here when I need you. I don't have anyone else in this world I can share these intimate fears with. No one else understands. They condemn and reject me." Perhaps psychotherapy, in the final analysis, is nothing more than a form of trained friendship! If so, then I am thankful for my calling. We critically need followers of the Master who can help others bear their burdens more easily through loving and honest relationships.

OBSTACLES TO CLOSE RELATIONSHIPS

Friendships are hard to develop and even harder to maintain. Many of the obstacles that prevent the formation of close relationships are the same as those that inhibit our happiness. I will briefly discuss three of them, just to underscore my main point of emphasis—that the development of close relationships rests entirely on you. You have no one else to blame if you lack friends.

The three obstacles to building friendships I will touch on are personality problems, self-hate, and faulty relationship style. As I review each of these, examine your own life carefully. See where you can identify weaknesses that need changing so you can be a better friend.

Personality Problems

Some personalities naturally work against the building of friend-ships. For instance, how many of the following traits describe you?

- Are you often taken as aloof, cool, detached, or uninterested in others?
- Do you find it easier to write than speak to someone?
- Do you tend to worry about what response you will give to someone who speaks to you?
- Do you rarely initiate social contact with anyone else?
- Do you often daydream about being the center of attraction and the life of the party?
- Do you always move to the outside of the circle of friends so as not to be noticed?
- Are you often labeled as timid and shy?

These characteristics are associated with the *introverted person-ality*. These traits can cause you to be blocked emotionally to the point that you cannot fulfill your actions and desires. Others may control you easily, and you may often feel wounded over being misunderstood. When this happens, you would usually prefer to steal away to lick your wounds all by yourself.

What about the following traits?

- Do you tend to see people as objects useful for meeting your needs?
- Do you find yourself not keeping promises or commitments?
- Are you easily angered when people block your way or frus-trate you?
- Do you prefer to make your own rules, rather than to abide by others' rules?
- Do you believe that lying is justified if it gets you out of trouble?
- Do you find it difficult to say you're sorry, even when you are clearly at fault?
- Do you see most other people as stupid, incompetent, or just not a match for you?

These characteristics go along with the *anti-social personality* and describe someone who sees little value in others and who tends to move from one relationship to another, always blaming others for the failure of the relationship.

Let us examine a third personality type:

- Do you lead a relatively normal life, but find yourself often suspecting the motives of others or distrusting their intentions?
- Do you often blame others for things that go wrong?
- Do you find it difficult to receive teasing?
- Do you prefer to keep your personal life secret and not allow others to know you intimately?
- Are you quick to question the loyalties of others?
- Are you jealous much of the time—either of your partner or of the successes of others?
- Do you have a short anger fuse?

If so, then you may have *paranoid personality* tendencies. You may be too focused on yourself, your safety, your reputation, and your success.

All three of these personality styles can work against the building of close relationships. They set up obstacles that may need to be removed before better friendships can be developed.

How can one set about changing these personality hindrances? *First* of all, it helps to understand those personality traits that may be hurting your ability to build relationships. Ask someone you trust to give you honest feedback—and really listen to what he or she has to say.

Second, if you begin to *behave* as you would like to, sooner or later you will begin to change. Of course, the quickest way to turn your personality quirks into healthy habits is to seek competent counseling. Deep-seated personality problems need expert and trained help to eradicate. Later in this chapter, I will describe the characteristics of a healthy personality. With determination you can begin to shape your personality to conform to these characteristics.

Self-hate

Another major hindrance to close relationships is a pervasive feeling that one is unlovable. You could feel this way because you consider yourself a dreadful person or because you think *others* see you as a terrible person. Either way, if you suffer from self-hate, you won't see any value in what you have to offer others, and therefore you will be unlikely to invest much effort in building relationships.

The person who feels self-hate will adopt any of several attitudes toward other people. He or she may make desperate efforts
to win affection, doing exceptional acts of kindness or loyalty and
then, when these efforts don't pay off, turning nasty and seeking
to hurt the one they are *trying to love*. Or such a person may
deliberately set up obstacles to relationships, perhaps by becoming excessively critical of others and always pointing out their
faults as a way of controlling or testing the relationship. "If he
cares for me, he won't mind if I point out his weakness" or "He'll
only respect me if I show him I know where his weaknesses are"
are typical self-statements.

Whatever the cause, the consequence is always the same—
people don't like you when you are full of self-hate. Your self-hate
makes them uncomfortable, and they often feel as if you don't
love them, either.

Self-hate has its origins in childhood and the adolescent years. It
can be deeply rooted and difficult to eradicate. The clearest prescription I know for curing it is found in Romans 12:3: "As God's
messenger I give each of you God's warning: Be honest in your
estimate of yourselves, measuring your value by how much faith
God has given you" (LB).

Honesty in how you think about yourself is essential for building self-esteem and repairing self-hate. In God's sight you are very
precious, so how can you think of yourself as having less value
than God places on you? Begin to reverse your self-hate by start-
ing to be honest in your estimate of yourself.

Poor Relationship Style

How do you relate to others? What is your "style"? Quite apart
from personality, each of us has a typical manner of relating to
others.

Eric Berne, in his landmark book, *Games People Play*,* identified four life positions which affect the styles we use in relating to
others. Understanding these positions has helped many people
develop a better understanding of how we can build better
friendships.

The first position is "I'm OK, You're OK" which Berne claims
is the healthiest. If you adopt this position, you treat everyone as
you want them to treat you; you relate as an equal. The other

---

* (New York: Ballantine, 1978).

styles are not as healthy. "I'm not OK, You're not OK" is a position of pessimism; it assumes both of us are inferior. "I'm not OK, You're OK" is the position of inferiority; it keeps you from opening up freely. "I'm OK, You're not OK" is the position of superiority. No one likes us when we think we are better than they are. These last three styles are almost guaranteed to damage or prevent relationships.

While these styles of seeing oneself in relation to others can be useful in explaining our attitude to others, they do not get to the heart of the matter. How should we think about ourselves in relation to others? The truth is that before God *none* of us is OK. It is only by His grace that we are restored to "OKness."

In clinical psychology or psychiatry, I suppose, we unconsciously adopt the position, "You're not OK; all we need now is to figure out why!" This is very unfair, because we all need God's grace and His regeneration at the core of our being.

Your style of relating, after you are made OK by God's restorative gospel, should always be one of deep respect and love for others. "There, but for the Grace of God, go I" should always be our position.

Quite apart from how you see yourself in relation to others (superior, inferior or equal) there are other "styles" that need to be avoided. For instance, trying to outsmart or outdo others never helps to build friendships. Most people resent this "competitive" style of relating. Also, you cannot expect others to get to know you if you don't share and disclose about yourself. This "secretive" style closes the doors to other people's hearts.

If you try excessively to please others, you may also hurt your relationships. You may attract some dependent and manipulative friends, but not genuine ones. Most of us really don't like people who constantly need to prove their love all the time through excessive kindness. On the other hand, an extremely independent and self-sufficient style can also alienate others. There needs to be a healthy balance between dependence and independence in all relationships. You must give as much as you expect to receive.

How can you know what your style of relating is? There's only one way: ask someone you trust to tell you. Be willing to receive that person's feedback and then consciously choose to change your behavior. It's not that difficult to behave in a different way if you really want to be a better friend. The next section will provide some practical suggestions.

OVERCOMING RELATIONSHIP PROBLEMS

Since deep, meaningful, and abiding relationships consistently produce happier people, we need to overcome whatever obstacles to intimacy lie in our way. The patterns that poison relationships can be identified and overcome. Here are some steps that can move you toward becoming a better friend:

(1) *Confront your relating style.* Don't be afraid to ask for feedback. Be courageous and open to hearing about your idiosyncracies.

(2) *Be willing to change those basic traits that inhibit intimacy.* Willingness to change is more than half the battle.

(3) *Begin to behave in the manner that you believe to be healthier.* Write out a description of how you would like to behave in a given relationship. Set down and memorize your intentions. Change always begins with the right behavior; feelings fall into line afterwards. Don't focus on the feelings, just do the right actions. Later on the new behavior will become second nature, and the feelings will come.

(4) *Do not attempt to reform or reprimand those with whom you are building a deeper relationship.* This is not your function. Focus only on your own need to change. As soon as you focus on the other person's need to change, the relationship will begin to deteriorate.

(5) *Choose your friendships carefully.* You cannot be close friends with everyone, only with those willing to reciprocate. Also, you cannot have equal intimacy with everyone. Select friends who respond to your intentions, share your values, and are willing to invest their time and commitment equally with you.

(6) *If a relationship is not "working," and if you have honestly and thoroughly reviewed your style or role and can sincerely say you are not the problem, move on to a new relationship.* It is a mistake to keep beating your head against the stone of an unyielding friend. Don't quit loving, just stop investing unnecessary time in someone who doesn't want to be a friend to you.

(7) *Even though you may have a few very special friends, make time for others also.* Widen the circle of your relationships. There are many lonely, shy, withdrawn, elderly, or difficult to reach people in God's world. You owe them some friendship, if only for a limited time and to a restricted depth. Develop a variety of relationships of differing degrees of intimacy. This makes for a rich and varied experience and opens up the door to friendships you never even thought about.

(8) *Don't repeat the mistakes of the past.* Every time a friendship fails, *learn* from it. Review it thoroughly, recording your mistakes for future reference. Take your desire to be a better friend seriously, and you will find it easier to change.

(9) *Work at keeping past relationships fresh.* Often we have to move on in life and leave old friends behind. When we leave high school or college, or move to a new neighborhood, we leave precious friendships behind. While new relationships are necessary, the old are also important. Nurture them with letters, phone calls, occasional visits, and periodic reunions. Think of them each as jewels in the crown of your happiness, and you will be richer than any king or queen who has ever reigned on this earth.

(10) *Keep God first in all your relationships.* No one should ever usurp His place. This should be your most intimate of all your relationships. "Ye are my friends," Jesus said, "if ye do whatsoever I command you" (John 15:14).

PRESCRIPTION FOR A LOVING PERSONALITY

Earlier in this chapter I described three personality types that work against the building of healthy relationships. Now let us consider the type of personality that facilitates intimacy. As I describe the traits that make up a perfect friend, you may wish to reflect on your own personality and select those qualities you would like to enhance in yourself.

- Do you love without coercion and without any expectation of reward?
- Do you embrace the feelings or opposing opinions of others without rejecting who they are as persons?
- Do you receive gifts or other expressions of love without embarrassment or false modesty?
- Do you safeguard the feelings and belongings of others as if they were your own?
- Do you promptly return something you have borrowed in respect for the one you borrowed it from?
- Do you go on loving someone who has hurt you without pulling away?
- Do you constantly work at overcoming prejudice or bias in order always to find the truth?
- Do you avoid getting bogged down in fits of anger, guilt, or self-blame?

- Do you generously give forgiveness to all who have intentionally or unintentionally harmed you?

If you do these loving things, you have a beautiful personality and are a treasure to all your friends. Not only will you be a happy person, but you will also shower happiness on others.

HELPFUL THOUGHTS

To be a friend . . .

- You must believe in others, acknowledging that they are as valuable to God as you are.
- You must strive to lift others up, not beat them down.
- You must be willing to give as much of yourself as you expect others to give to you.
- You must be as interested in helping others fulfill their dreams and goals as you are in fulfilling your own.
- You must be a good listener and be willing to choose silence.
- You may have to stop giving advice and focus on understanding others.
- You must be willing sometimes to close your eyes to the faults of others and ignore their reactions.
- You must set aside hypocrisy, artificiality, and all pretense to be greater than you are.
- You must value truthfulness and honesty.
- You must always be willing to take the first step toward reconciliation.
- You can do no better than model yourself after the Greatest Friend anyone can have—Jesus Himself.

"Henceforth I call you not servants; for the servant knoweth not what his Lord doeth; but I have called you friends . . ." (John 15:15).

Happiness Is Having the
Right Attitudes

JUST A FEW WEEKS AGO, I was watching a program on our local public television station. It was the life story of the famous dancer and choreographer, Agnes De Mille. As the niece of Cecil B. De Mille, producer of many famous movie epics including *The Ten Commandments*, Agnes struggled for years to achieve recognition in her own right. Finally in 1928 she went to London and became a hit when she choreographed the first American ballet, *Rodeo*. She went on to give the world such outstanding choreography as the dance sequences in *Brigadoon* and *Paint Your Wagon*, and the brilliant dream sequences that made the movie *Oklahoma* a classic bit of Americana. This gifted woman was felled with a stroke while waiting for the curtain to go up on one of her productions. The damage was severe, and her painful but persistent struggle to learn to walk and speak all over again late in life was vividly captured by the TV documentary. Finally Agnes De Mille did walk and talk again—a triumph for the human spirit.

Reflecting on the consequences of her apparent disaster, the interviewer asked Agnes what the whole experience had done to her. Almost without hesitation she replied, "It has made me a happier person. I am more tranquil now than I have ever been—more contented."

Immediately I was reminded of a very important principle of happiness: *It is not what happens to you, but your attitude toward the happening, that determines your happiness.*

It is probably very hard to accept this truth when you are suffering from an unpleasant or catastrophic life experience. I am very aware that even as I write, many readers are being dragged through an unwanted divorce or some other painful situation they did not choose. Others are struggling to survive financially or even are facing bankruptcy. And still others are agonizing over

a son or daughter who is in trouble. Some are forcing themselves
to go to work daily, facing drudgery or an unsympathetic supervi-
sor. I know all about these struggles because I try to help people
like this every day of my life. And yet, I repeat: It is not what
happens to you, but your attitude toward it, that determines your
happiness.

Happiness is *independent* of our life's circumstances. *It has to be!*
Otherwise, there is no hope at all for any happiness. What is important is developing the right attitude toward all of our predica-
ments and conflict situations.

THE RIGHT ATTITUDES

What attitudes create happiness? Can we develop them in our
minds? The answer to the second question is definitely "yes." The
first requires further exploration.

I have already mentioned the Beatitudes that Jesus relates in
Matthew 5:1-12. The word *blessed* really means "happy," but with
a very special connotation: It is a happiness that comes from the
purest of all motives. It is extremely important that we seek happiness in the way that Jesus intended us to.

The remarkable point about this list of things Jesus says can
bring us happiness is that to the Jews they all represented God's
curses.

Yes! Examine each of the Beatitudes again, and as you do so
remember that every one of them was viewed as a curse. "Poor in
Spirit," "mourning," "meekness," "hunger," "persecution," and so
forth were not aspects of life that any Jew enjoyed or sought after.
From the moment of birth, little Jewish children were taught to
avoid these signs of God's disfavor and to believe that the *only* sign
of God's blessing was the sign of material prosperity in every shape
and form. But Jesus turned them around and declares that happiness is to be found even in these apparent curses. Why? Because
blessing resides in our attitude to life's traumas.

At first glance, the Beatitudes seem like just a list of beautiful
sentiments. In reality they are startling observations. They are dy-
namite, charged with all the power of the Holy Ghost to explode
our preconceptions and revolutionize our lives. Behind them is the
love of God, longing to transform our pain into peaceful rest and
our struggling into serene trust. Turn your attitudes over to the
Divine Physician, and He will heal them of their thorns and neu-
tralize the poison that blocks your happiness.

One of the important themes that stands out in the Beatitudes is that you cannot get back from life more than you put into it. Matthew 5:6–9 emphasizes this. You cannot treat people in a way that makes *them* unhappy and then expect to find happiness yourself. The universal law of happiness is that "you reap what you sow." You sow *first* ("hunger for righteousness," "mercy," "peace-making"), and then you reap happiness later.

It's even more critical than this. As any farmer will tell, you reap *more* than you sow. So if you dispense disrespect, unkindness, and unforgiveness, you will receive back much more of these terrible things than you expected. By the same token, the person who dispenses the positive characteristics of the Beatitudes will reap blessings many times over. You must treat people well if you want to be well treated.

ATTITUDES AND OUR THINKING

All attitudes are ultimately the product of our thinking, so we need to take a moment to reflect on how they are formed in our thought life.

When we use the term *attitude*, we are referring to the overall tendency we have to respond to people, objects, or circumstances in a certain way. Our response can be positive (we like what we see and want more of it) or negative (we hate it and want to avoid it). Attitudes are *learned* through experience and are made up of feelings, thoughts, and actions.

The best news of all is that attitudes can be changed! How? By changing the way we think about things. Feelings and actions will follow if we first change our thoughts.

You will never be a happy person until you begin to *think* like one. If you are unhappy at this moment, put down this book (after reading the rest of this paragraph), close your eyes, and begin to think of some pleasant past experience in your life. See how quickly you begin to feel the emotion of happiness return? Now reverse the experiment—think of something unpleasant, and see how quickly your unhappiness returns. Prove to yourself that "thinking determines how you feel."

On a trip to New York a few weeks ago, I was feeling a little down. It had been a heavy, demanding week, and I was tired. As usual when I am fatigued, I began to dwell on the unpleasant issues of my life.

A movie came on the screen in the jumbo jet, so I decided to watch it, if only to be distracted. It was an interesting story of two totally different men and their problems with women. For the one it was his mother, and the other his wife. Together they became linked in a slapstick comedy of misunderstandings and plans that go awry.

In the middle of the story there is a very touching scene (it was almost out of place in the whole movie). Both men are sitting at breakfast depressed and miserable. Their plans have all gone wrong; everything was a mess. The simple-minded, clumsy son of a domineering and crotchety old mother goes to the corner of the room, lifts a floorboard, and pulls out a metal box. He lies on the floor, opens the box, and invites his intelligent and sophisticated companion to examine his coin collection. At first his friend declines, then agrees to look at the coins.

They lie together on the floor, coins spread all around them. Expecting to see rare and expensive coins, the friend is disappointed as he realizes that they are just common, everyday coins—pennies, dimes, and quarters with no great value.

But then the simple-minded clutz begins to recount the meaning of each coin. Before his death, his father had allowed him to keep the change whenever they went somewhere together. "This penny was the change from an ice-cream vendor at Disneyland." "This quarter I got to keep at a movie." Every coin was accounted for with great affection—every detail recalled. Never had he spent a coin that had a connection with his late father; he had saved every one of them.

And suddenly you got the message: this man had loved his father very deeply, and these coins were the symbols of that love. They were links to a rich storehouse of happy memories which he could recall at any time, even though his present life with an aging and grumpy mother was miserable.

Then I remembered that I also have a metal box full of coins. And they too are not valuable treasures, but "memory symbols"—coins my grandfather had given me from the Boer War or that were associated with places I'd been to. As I sat there in my plane seat, I recalled two small Italian coins that were change from a vendor at the Colosseum in Rome. Another was change from a boat on a trip round Lake Geneva. I have an English penny I picked up near the simple, country-church grave of Winston Churchill, a man I have admired greatly from my childhood recollections of the Second World War.

And suddenly, thinking of my coins and my memories, I

no longer felt miserable. As I remembered my rich storehouse of happy memories, my attitude to my present circumstances changed, and that flight to New York became a happy time. I had so much to be thankful for that my present uncomfortable and unhappy circumstances faded into insignificance.

All one needs to recover the feeling of happiness is to focus your thoughts on things that will produce happiness. Unpleasant incidents in your life, once they have been dealt with, are in the past, so let them stay there. If you find yourself dragging them out in moments of discomfort, put them back where they belong. Don't let them destroy the happiness of the present.

The future can also be a problem. Fearful thoughts about what might or might not happen can extinguish our capacity for happiness and debilitate our spirits. Even here, remembering happy events and being thankful for the faithfulness of God, family, and friends in the past and present can help to ease the painfulness of anxiety about the future.

WHAT ATTITUDES CREATE HAPPINESS?

Except in rare instances, happiness does not simply fall from heaven. Because we live in a world fraught with unavoidable misfortune, illness, struggles, poverty, and conflicts ready to overtake us when we least expect it, we need to develop the "right" attitudes ahead of these times. By reflection and careful attention to our thought processes, we can understand our present attitudes and then deliberately set about to change them. Fortunately, God is eager to help us in this process.

Since most of us are not rich, nor were we born with good natures or peaceful hearts, happiness must be something we achieve through effort and determination. The amount of effort it will take depends largely on the ease with which we can change our attitudes.

What attitudes should we develop in order to better prepare ourselves for the crises of life? I want to suggest five for your prayerful consideration:

An Attitude That Turns Miserable Circumstances into Tolerable Ones

James 1:2–3 has a very important message for us: "Count it all joy, my brethren, when you meet various trials, for you know that the testing of your faith produces steadfastness" (RSV). I want to focus on the phrase, "count it all joy." It literally means "turn it around," "make it into," or "consider it as done"! This implies that you can make of circumstances what you want, that you can look your problems in the face and say, "This is most unfortunate; I wish it wasn't happening to me right now, but since it is I will make the best I can of it and turn it into something joyful." Miserable circumstances are then made into tolerable circumstances.

When we do this, we build character, maturity, and steadfastness. If we don't, we perpetuate a state of misery. The choice is ours!

Every now and again I try to bake bread. I will confess that I envy those who can bake french bread that is crispy on the outside, fluffy and full of little holes on the inside. My attempts always end up flat and solid. And it's not for want of trying. I've tried my hand at baking ever since we got married, and I haven't succeeded yet. It has become a family joke. One daughter calls the other and says, "Guess what Dad is doing?" and almost without hesitation the reply is, "Baking bread again, is he?"

Well, I don't intend to give up. And one reason I keep trying is that my wife has taught me how to turn my bread failures into the most delicious bread pudding. The greater the bread flop, the better the pudding! Failures and miserable life circumstances *can* be turned into delicious morsels of growth. It is all a matter of attitude.

An Attitude That Places Catastrophe in Perspective

We lose our happiness when we lose perspective. When we cannot see the significance of the whole, we become disoriented, and even little disappointments can cause major unhappiness.

All of life involves loss. From the day we are born to the day we die, we are gaining and losing. In every stage of life, we leave behind friends and opportunities. Finally, we all die. God intended life on earth to be this way; He never promised otherwise. The ability to see the whole—from God's point of view and to the best of our ability—is necessary for happiness and sanity.

First Corinthians 13:12 reminds us that "For now we see through a glass, darkly; but then face to face: now I know in part; but then shall I know even as also I am known." We cannot know all the answers to the questions and paradoxes of life this side of heaven, but we *must* seek to put all our experiences into the perspective of eternity.

To have this perspective means that we know:

- *who* we are before God.
- *where* we are going in His plan.
- *why* we do the things we do.

It means that we have a clear plan and direction for our lives so that each apparent catastrophe can be seen in the context of the whole.

Unless you have laid such a foundation in your thinking, it is hard to maintain perspective.

In my mid-twenties, I experienced a major catastrophe. As an engineer I had re-enrolled in the university part-time to do an advanced course in mathematics. I wanted to be able to create more sophisticated structural designs than I was doing.

Now, my mathematics background was quite impressive. I had won a national prize in high school and had always found complicated subjects a challenge. So I was not particularly worried about the outcome of the course.

At the end of a whole year of study, I went to take the examination. It was pass or fail, and a whole year of work depended on my handling of that exam. I tore the envelope open and hurriedly selected the questions I would answer. But after two or three pages of calculations on the first question I realized I wasn't succeeding. So I moved quickly to the next—and bombed out on it, too.

By the end of the first hour I was devastated. For the first time in my life, I was failing an examination. I gave up after another half an hour, and in a deep depression walked aimlessly about the campus, too ashamed to go home and tell my wife of the disaster.

Shortly afterwards I enrolled in a course in psychology, and a whole new interest began to emerge that eventually took my life in a totally different direction. Now, when I reflect back on that examination failure I ask myself, "Was that really a catastrophe?" I must confess that it still is not one of my favorite memories. But I also have to admit that in the long run the experience was positive, because it was that apparent failure which turned me to a new career as a clinical psychologist. Now, of course, I would not have it otherwise, and I constantly remind myself that apparent catastrophe is not always what it seems to be.

An Uncomplaining Attitude

One of the difficult facts we must accept in life is that genuine accomplishments rarely happen when we need them most. They emerge only after a long struggle, usually about the time we are ready to give up. Now, since most of us dislike prolonged periods of conflict or struggle, we tend to seek the easiest outlet available to us during these times—complaining.

Now complaining, whether it takes the form of "dumping" on a spouse, using a friend as a scapegoat, or whining in prayer to God, may seem to give momentary relief, but in the long run it builds an attitude that works against you.

For one thing, complaining tends to alienate other people. After all, who likes to be around someone who is always griping and whining? If we fall in the habit of constantly complaining, friends tend to pull away, withdrawing the very support we so desperately need.

Complaining also weakens our defenses against further problems. It uses up energy that could be used in attacking problems creatively and seeking solutions. And because it keeps our focus trained on the negative aspects of the situation, it makes us less likely to see the positives—the possibilities for growth and change.

An Attitude That Resists Blaming

Many psychologists believe, as I do, that the more we engage in blaming, the more turmoil we experience, and the less capable we are of remedying a problem.

There are several reasons for this. The primary one is that blaming ourselves or others for mistakes and wrongdoing detracts from the real issues that need attention. Our time and energy is consumed with finding and punishing the "culprit" (even ourselves) instead of taking steps to fix the problem. Besides, this need to pinpoint people as the source of every problem blinds us to the fact that many problems result from accidents or chance circumstances. And naturally we cannot fix a problem if we don't even recognize the nature of the problem.

Another reason blaming causes turmoil is that it is an outward symptom of an inability to accept imperfection in ourselves and others. We assign blame because we do not have the courage to be human or the grace to allow others the right to make mistakes. And since we live in an imperfect world, this attitude is bound to make us continually unhappy.

Emotionally disturbed people often have a deeply entrenched need to blame and therefore spend a lot of time fault-finding and criticizing. They compulsively place the focus of wrongdoing on "who did what" instead of taking the steps to change the behavior that caused the problem in the first place.

Blaming also makes us unhappy because it sets up barriers in our intimate relationships. Blame feels like an attack; the natural response to being blamed for a problem is to defend ourselves—and possibly cast the blame elsewhere—not to find a way to remedy the problem. And so an attitude of blaming can set up a pattern of attack and counterattack that turns a relationship into a battleground.

Parents can easily get caught up in this attitude trap, especially when their children are in the adolescent stage. "Johnny, it's your fault the tire went flat. You used the car last." (No allowance is made for the fact that the tire was already well-worn by the rest of the family.) "Mary, you must have done something wrong. Otherwise your friends wouldn't have turned on you." (No allowance is made for the possibility that the friends might be inconsiderate or selfish.) Many teenagers feel the injustice of this attitude and eventually reject what their parents stand for.

I believe blame and censure are the motivating forces behind much adolescent rebellion and are also the main destructive forces in many unhappy marriages. An attitude of blame is almost guaranteed to destroy happiness in almost any close relationship.

An Attitude of Thankfulness

All unhappiness depends to some degree on a feeling of dissatisfaction with what one is achieving or receiving from life. Unhappiness results from the belief that we are losing—or at least not succeeding as well as others are.

Most of us are creatures of comparison, and we have difficulty accepting the successes of others when we don't feel very successful ourselves. But when we fall into this attitude of comparing ourselves with others—or when we feel "entitled" to a painless, disappointment-free existence, we lose the spirit of thankfulness—and if there is one attitude that is indispensable to happiness, it is this attitude of thankfulness.

Thankfulness is very important for spiritual growth. The psalmist tells us that it is a prerequisite for worship: "Enter into his gates with thanksgiving, and into his courts with praise: be thankful unto him, and bless his name" (Ps. 100:4). The apostle Paul advised the church at Thessalonica: "In everything give thanks; for this is the will of God in Christ Jesus concerning you" (1 Thess. 5:18). Thankfulness is an essential part of being a Christian.

And yet thanksgiving does not come naturally. There are no genes for it, nor is there a "thankfulness center" in our brains. Thankfulness has to be deliberately developed by maintaining an acute awareness of what is good in life. The practice of thankfulness is a matter of constantly "counting your blessings."

There are three foci of thankfulness—God, others, and yourself. None should be neglected. Make it a habit to be conscious of every good thing in your life. Savor each blessing. Begin your day by reviewing all you have to be thankful for. Light each hour with gratitude. When twilight falls and the toils of your day are done—again count your blessings. Lift them up so they stand above the shadows of your hardships. If you do this often, your blessings will light your heart with happiness, and your dreams will be sweet.

Count your blessings while you have the strength and ability to do it. Our time on this earth is short, and lovely things abound, just waiting for our touch and appreciation. Big or small, whatever comes your way, receive it thankfully from the hand of God, and you will find that your world is a place of love and divine blessing.

HELPFUL THOUGHTS

Thanking God

- *Thank God* for the gift of life and live it triumphantly.
- *Thank God* for your special gifts and abilities. Dedicate them to His service.
- *Thank God* for opportunities and challenges that make work possible and dreams fulfilling.
- *Thank God* for each new day by living it to the fullest.

Thanking Others

- *Thank someone special* today for their love and consideration.
- *Thank your friends* for their faithfulness and willingness to tolerate you.
- *Thank your parents*, even if they are departed, for the life they gave you.

- *Thank your spouse*, children, or other relatives for the happiness they share with you.

Thanking Yourself

- *Thank yourself* for patience and a willingness to allow yourself to be imperfect.
- *Thank yourself* for the gift of forgiveness that you can share with yourself and others.
- *Thank yourself* for a willingness to be honest with yourself and purposely to overcome a state of unhappiness.
- *Thank yourself* for just being yourself, for the beauty God is creating within and the happiness you can radiate without.

PRINCIPLE FIFTEEN

Happiness Is Praying "Thy Will Be Done"

I BELIEVE THIS to be the hardest of all the happiness principles to put into practice. It is as hard to understand as it is to implement, as difficult to grasp as it is to apply. But no matter how difficult it may seem, praying "Thy will be done" has a very important part to play in your mastery of happiness. Unless you can take this final step, you will have come within final grasp of what it means to live to the fullest, yet still missed God's best for you.

Happiness comes from the "heart"—that deep part of us that we think of as the center of our being. In this palpitating core of our spirit, we find an affinity with all that God provides for our healing and sustenance. And only when we learn to pray "Thy will be done" at all times and under all circumstances can we truly tune our hearts to His.

That kind of relationship is hinted at in John 1:47, where Jesus said of Nathaniel, "Behold an Israelite indeed, in whom there is no guile" (John 1:47). Without guile—what a beautiful way to describe a person! It seems to picture someone whose heart is true to God, who has such complete trust and willingness to obey that these qualities show on his face. Here is a mind that sought only to discover and do God's will. *This* is a happy heart. And this is a heart that grows from praying "Thy will be done."

The phrase, "Thy will be done," primarily comes from the Lord's Prayer quoted in Matthew 6:10, although Jesus prayed it again in the Garden of Gethsemane just before the crucifixion. As you will recall, He left His disciples and went a little further into the Garden where He fell on His face and prayed, "O my Father, if it be possible, let this cup pass from me: nevertheless not as I will, but as Thou wilt" (Matt. 26:39). James, possibly remembering this prayer of Jesus, makes it a rule of life when he tells us, "For that ye ought to say, If the Lord will, we shall live, and do this, or that" (James 4:15).

171

Jesus was not afraid of doing the will of God; He never wavered from His commitment to fulfilling it. His own will was set aside in Gethsemane as He followed God to the cross, the way of victory. He never shirked His responsibility.

"Thy will be done" is a prayer of *complete submission* and *total obedience*. No one can be totally happy who does not come to the place where he or she can pray it. Because the master key for happiness is meeting the challenge of each new day with the serene faith that "all things work together for good to them that love God, to them who are the called according to his purpose" (Rom. 8:28).

THE NEED FOR MATURITY

All happiness must move us to a greater maturity, not a lesser one. It should reveal to us the balance we must achieve between that which can be changed and that which ought not be changed because God wills it be so.

As someone who has had for many years a first-hand look at people's personal problems, I would say that *more maturity* is one of our greatest needs. No matter what culture I encounter, I see immature people attempting to handle mature problems—children playing at being adults. And the more sophisticated the culture becomes, the greater the level of technological advancement, the less able people seem to be to deal with the basic problems of living—problems that desperately need a dose of maturity to fix them.

Take the parenting task as an example. No one really knows what to do anymore—or so it seems. Simple discipline is hard to achieve because parents feel so insecure about doing the wrong thing. Plain common sense is immobilized as a result of pseudo-scientific beliefs about the ways we can harm our kids. A common interpretation of much pop psychology warns us, "Don't make your kids angry at you" or "If you allow them to feel too much anxiety, they'll become neurotic." Parents aren't allowed to be themselves, so their kids can't become their true selves—and later won't be able to be themselves with their own children. We can certainly do with some basic maturity and common sense as parents. And this goes for so many aspects of our lives.

We need maturity in order to be happy. We need simple wisdom for living. We need to feel less afraid of making mistakes and more freedom to take risks. We need to balance our lives with large doses of plain common sense. But above all, we need the maturity that faith in our God can bring to us. If we do not consciously and deliberately seek this maturity, we will become preoccupied with the petty issues of life, self-stunted and unhappy.

We were made for maturity. We were created to become full-grown adults physically, psychologically, and spiritually. Anything that stunts our growth will produce unhappiness.

Now, I don't mean to imply that we must be equally mature in every aspect of our beings. We will all have "pockets of immaturity"—attitudes, emotional reactions, or behaviors that resemble those of five- or six-year-olds. We may regress periodically to some childish habit or prejudice, or an adult jealousy may have its roots in infantile fantasy. But occasional immaturity in a few areas is not necessarily a problem. We need to give each other permission to outgrow such immature areas.

I also don't mean to imply that we must all grow to maturity at the same speedy rate. Just as we mature physically at different speeds, our rates of achieving psychological and spiritual maturity may differ also. Some of us may still be struggling with basic temper control while others have moved on to mastering more complex life issues. What is important is that we continue to move toward maturity, no matter how slowly. If you are stunted or halted in your growth—or perhaps slipping backwards—you may be in need of an extra dose of spiritual growth hormone!

A PRAYER OF MATURITY

What does the prayer, "Thy will be done," have to do with growing to maturity? A lot! It is the prayer that feeds all growth, both in one's spirit and in one's psyche. God specializes in maturity. His central aim is to produce in us maturity of character and faith as well as a congenial spirit. Read Ephesians 4:11–14:

> And he gave some, apostles; and some, prophets; . . . for the perfecting of the saints, for the work of the ministry, for the edifying of the body of Christ: Till we all come . . . unto a perfect man, unto the measure of the stature of the fulness of Christ: That we henceforth be no more children, tossed to and fro . . .

Everything God has provided—the evangelist who brought you to Christ; the brothers and sisters who discipled you, prayed for you, taught you; the work of His Spirit in you—is focused toward one goal: your maturing and reaching the stature of the fullness of Christ.

When you pray, "Thy will be done," you are offering a prayer of complete submission, total surrender. You are saying, "Lord, just as Jesus struggled in Gethsemane over whether to drink His cup of bitterness and asked that if possible the cup should pass from Him, so I pray for this painful thing confronting me to pass away. Nevertheless, I am willing to accept whatever your will is in this matter."

This is the *highest* form of prayer because it recognizes that God knows better than you. It is the *happiest* form of prayer because it is the prayer of complete surrender to a God you acknowledge as all-loving and desirous of only the best for your life. It is the *healthiest* form of prayer because it invites you to subject yourself to God's will, whatever that may be—and His will is always good for you.

Most important of all, praying this prayer gives you a significant opportunity for growth in your relationship with God. After all, God will do His will whether or not we pray "Thy will be done." But praying this way opens up our minds and hearts to following Him. We are the losers if we cannot do it.

WE ARE AFRAID OF THIS PRAYER

I believe that deep down most of us are afraid to pray "Thy will be done" for ourselves. (It is always easy enough to pray it for others!) Perhaps we are confronted with losing a loved one or failing significantly in business, and we pray about it. But often, the more painful the circumstance, the more we resist praying "Thy will be done." Why? We hesitate because we think that God may not want to do for us what we want to do for ourselves. What if it isn't His will that my beloved be healed or this catastrophe be averted! What if He prefers me to learn patience from my pain? Perhaps it's better that I don't pray "Thy will be done," but ask for what I really want!

I try not to argue with God anymore! There was a time, in my youth, when I thought I knew better than God what I needed in my life. As I've become more mature (in age if nothing else), I've come to see that my paltry wisdom pales into insignificance against God's great wisdom. Events I have desperately wanted to happen a certain way have turned out better because they happened differently. I am glad some of my prayers were never answered the way I wanted them to be. Most times in my life it would have been better for me to have prayed, "Thy will be done."

Let me suggest some further reasons we are afraid of this prayer. First, and very simply, *we're not totally sure that God's will is best for us*. Perhaps we are afraid that somehow God will forget or overlook what is His best will for us—or that He arbitrarily dishes out unhappiness "just to shape us up."

How often we hear statements like "I haven't gotten over my son's dying on his sixteenth birthday yet. But I suppose it was God's will, so I must accept it." Or "My mother died of cancer when she was only fifty. But it must have been God's will." Isn't it odd how we always seem to associate God's will with some tragedy? It's as if we think He awards a drowning here, a cancer there, or a devastating flood in the next county just to accomplish His purposes! What a tragic view of how God works in our lives. Such a view feeds our fear of "God's will" and frightens us away from praying "Thy will be done."

We need to understand that God's will *is always the best there is for us*—and that includes good things! Most human tragedy is the consequence of human actions or poor decisions, not God's punishment or divine purposes. We all suffer from the evil loose in the world. Let us not blame God for it!

Another reason I think we fear to pray "Thy will be done" is *we are afraid that if we are not very specific and absolutely positive about what we pray for*, God won't hear us. We tend to give God human characteristics. Because people don't listen well, we fear that God doesn't, either. But God not only hears what we very specifically say, He also knows what we need but fail to pray for. Perhaps our parents were difficult listeners, but let us not reduce God to their limitations.

Third, *we are afraid that God will use every bad circumstance to punish or discipline us*. We assume His "will" is to correct, not give us joy—or so we believe. Here again, we reduce God to human qualities. Our feelings about parents and other authority figures transfer to God, and it becomes hard to separate our suspicions of people from our fear that God wants to punish us. We easily slip into thinking that somehow God wants revenge more than He wants to forgive or heal—after all, this is how people have treated us.

Praise God, He is not like us—or our parents, our friends, or like any human we know! He *can* be trusted. His will is always best—so we can pray with great confidence "Thy will be done!"

Fourth, *we are afraid to pray this prayer because it means that we surrender our will to God's*. It's part of our ongoing struggle for control and autonomy. "Why can't I have it my way?" "What's wrong with my plan for my life?" "I know what I need better than anyone else does."

We are by nature rebellious. Disobedience is a symptom of our need for independence and autonomy. This is why so many of us rebel as teenagers—we feel the need to assert our autonomy, and we see rebellion as a symbol of freedom and of self-government. And most of us never really outgrow this need for "self-power." For many it emerges again at the mid-life stage when men and women with a history of otherwise mature and responsible behavior suddenly throw all control to the wind and become rebellious again, discarding morals and running away to newfound lovers or from old responsibilities. The rebelliousness was there all the time; it just lacked a reason and opportunity for expression.

This potential for rebelliousness is also always there toward God. Don't be fooled by your calm and obedient exterior. You may seem to be "well-surrendered" and obedient, but believe me the day could easily come when, as a result of some special temptation, trauma, or disaster, your "rebellious button" could be pushed. It will then be very hard for you to pray "Thy will be done."

Don't ignore the rebellious part of your nature; it might explode unexpectedly. Instead, as you seek to grow in spiritual maturity, always praying "Thy will be done," also pray that God will keep you in touch with your struggle to be obedient and that He will give you His power to surrender to His will. Without God's help in doing this, you will always be on the verge of mutiny.

TWO WAYS TO PRAY "THY WILL BE DONE"

We can pray this prayer in two ways. One is rooted in despair, the other in hope and happiness.

The first way is to pray, "OK, I know there's no hope in this situation. So, God, please just have your way. I am resigned to it."

The second way is, "My God, I know you always desire the best for me. My trust is in You; please do Your will in me."

The first is bad; the second is good. The first drives us away from God; the second draws us to Him: Both are forms of resignation to God's will, but the two have significantly different consequences.

The resignation of the first is an act of hopelessness and discouragement. We pray it when we are depressed and dejected, when we resign ourselves to the inevitable worst outcome. I am only thankful that when God hears us pray this form of resignation, He understands the deep hurts of our heart that produce it. In His mercy He transforms this prayer into one of hope.

The resignation of the second form of this prayer is an act of faith. We pray it because unconquerable hope beats in our breast. We know that "all things work together for good." Despite the facts that we will all eventually be defeated by death (because it is in the will of God that we cannot live forever), or that our enemies will constantly seek to harm us, we accept our circumstances and submit ourselves to whatever purpose God seeks to accomplish. This is a sure foundation for happiness.

Such a prayer of faith does not waste time attempting to change unchangeable circumstances, nor does it seek to avoid the unavoidable. Rather than fretting and becoming furious, it fastens onto the will of God as the only source of constancy and security. It helps us hold fast to a solid anchor for all of life's storms.

When "Thy will be done" is prayed with real understanding and deep conviction, it becomes a prayer of great wisdom and depth, because it attempts to tune in to God's mind and seeks only to give expression to His purposes.

WHY SHOULD WE PRAY "THY WILL BE DONE"?

When we pray "Thy will be done," we accomplish a number of things, all of which contribute to our basic feeling of well-being and happiness:

- *We demonstrate that we can trust the God we claim to be our Savior.* Those who see our faith will be drawn to Him through this trust.
- *We reveal our understanding that all of life is finally under the control of God*—and that even while we do not see a purpose in all its shadows now, we will one day.
- *We place all our troubles under God's protection,* claiming that the blood of Christ has redeemed all that is sinful and restored all that is not whole.
- *We demonstrate our understanding of the role suffering plays in God's redemptive plan.* We cannot grow without suffering, and we miss a great part of God's blessing when we fail to participate with Him in tribulation.
- *We free ourselves of unnecessary worry and anxiety.* If God's will is being done, then why should we fret and rage? If His

purpose is being worked out—whether through apparent failure, unexplainable sickness, or other circumstance—why would we oppose it?

- *We avoid wasting energy on trivial problems.* We can see the "whole" much better and understand how God works in *all* of our life.
- *We confront our own desires and face the truth about ourselves.* Even though this may be painful, even humiliating, in the final analysis it is indispensable to a lasting happiness. Praying "Thy will be done" and applying it specifically to our own personalities cannot fail to revolutionize our lives.

HELPFUL THOUGHTS

I began this chapter by emphasizing that "Thy will be done" is the most mature of all prayers. Since this prayer touches the very center of God's purposes for us, there can be no greater act of surrender than to pray it sincerely.

But this prayer not only is mature; it *creates maturity* over time in those who pray it often. You can prove this for yourself. Begin to pray "Thy will be done" on a regular basis. Whenever you ask God for something, qualify your prayer with "nevertheless, let Your will be done!" I believe you will quickly see a remarkable maturity emerge in both your feelings and behavior. Here are some of the maturity changes likely to occur:

- You will be guided more by long-term purposes than immediate desires.
- You will come to accept things and people for what they are—not what you want them to be.
- You will more easily come to accept the authority of others, without rebellion or self-abdication.
- You will find criticism less painful to receive and more beneficial to your growth.
- You will be better able to work without being a slave to your work and to play without feeling guilty.
- You will find loving others easier and receiving love less important.
- You will discover that God has His hand on all your life. While you may not immediately see His purposes being worked out, in due time you will marvel at His consistent care of you.

POSTSCRIPT

Why Not Be a Ten?

IN MY PREFACE I asked you to rate your level of happiness on a scale from 0 to 10 and to remember your score. It has been my prayer that, as you have progressed through this book, you have discovered ways to be a happier person, and that you have identified and disposed of the many obstacles to your happiness.

All that remains is for me to encourage you to strive to be a "ten" as often as you can. I know from personal experience that the careful and consistent application of the principles I have outlined in these pages will go a long way toward making you happier. I claim no profound philosophical depth for what has been written, but I can attest to its practical value. These common-sense principles can revolutionize your life if you will apply them in the context of your Christian faith.

I am left with a vague feeling that there are some things I haven't said or that I did not intend to be taken in the way they have been. To ensure that my ideas on how to build a happier disposition have not been misleading and to make up for my lack of precision at some points, I would like to use these closing paragraphs to "batten down the hatches."

First of all, I never at any point intended to imply that we can constantly and unchangingly be happy. Never-ending happiness is for fairy tales. We cannot live "happily ever after," no matter how perfectly we follow all the right rules. It is in the nature of human experience that there will be ups and downs, point and counterpoint, sunrises and sunsets, all the days of our lives!

Sorrow, sadness, pain, and depression all have value in this life. Their purpose is clear: they help us to understand and plumb the full depth of human emotion, teach us valuable lessons of right and wrong, protect us from harm, and help us grieve our losses.

179

But these emotions, necessary as they are to our existence, are qualitatively different from the day-to-day, ordinary unhappiness from which we suffer. The challenge I leave with you is to find deep happiness and joy even in your afflictions.

I also never intended to give the impression that all we need for achieving happiness resides within the human spirit. I am far from being a humanist! To be honest, if I thought that happiness was entirely a human endeavor, I wouldn't have bothered to write this book. But I have taken up this task because I sincerely believe that our general level of day-to-day happiness could be greater if we understood how the gospel facilitates our joy. In order to be truly happy, we need not loftier ideals nor more sophisticated intelligence, but a more complete surrender of our wills to God's will. The majority of us are hibernating through life when we could be living in the full sunlight of all God's provisions.

The person who lives in this sunlight feels like a citizen of God's kingdom and freely enjoys all the privileges and liberties of such an inhabitant. In this profound union of creature and Creator, real happiness simply cannot be disrupted!